COMMON SENSE AND THE CURRICULUM

Common Sense and the Curriculum

ROBIN BARROW
MA (Oxon.), PhD (London)

LINNET BOOKS
HAMDEN, CONNECTICUT

First published 1976 by George Allen & Unwin Ltd.
London, and in The United States of America
as a LINNET BOOK, an imprint of
The Shoe String Press, Inc., Hamden, Connecticut.

Library of Congress Cataloging in Publication Data

Barrow, Robin.
   Common sense and the curriculum.

   Includes index.
   1. Curriculum planning. 1. Title.
LB1570.B328   375'.001   75-43540
ISBN 0-208-01590-6

Printed in Great Britain

To the Family

'I have said what needs to be said. If people do not like me for it, I shall be unpopular.'
U. Terque: *Evil and Absurdity*

'I am a philosopher. I think and write, I suppose, as a philosopher. But as to whether what I actually say is philosophical – to that I am supremely indifferent. I am only interested in truth, good reason and common sense. And the greatest of these is common sense.'
Hannah Ball: *Evil and Absurdity*

Contents

Introduction

This book was written backwards. It came into being to meet a specific query raised about my previous book, *Moral Philosophy for Education*, raised by two tolerant but shrewd critics. In that book I argued that 'an activity is worthwhile insofar as it promotes pleasure and/or diminishes pain in general'[1] and that, consequently, 'the task of education is . . . broadly speaking, to develop people in such a way that they will be enabled to take pleasure in life, while contributing to the maximisation of pleasure in the community as a whole. What is educationally worthwhile is whatever will contribute to that end.'[2] Both Ivor Morrish and Peter Renshaw, independently, suggested to me that, even if one accepted my argument so far, it led in practice to the conclusion that virtually anything could be educationally worthwhile. They felt, perhaps, that there were certain things that I would regard as educationally worthwhile, which would not necessarily be so by my argument. They wanted a clearer account of what kind of curriculum my theory would actually lead to and why.

It suited my purpose very well to oblige. For not only did it seem to me that the theory did not lead to the conclusion that virtually anything could be educationally worthwhile, but it also occurred to me that if I could convincingly outline and justify a specific curriculum, in the light of my utilitarian premiss, two purposes would be served. First, I would answer their query, but secondly I would gain plausibility for my thesis: if it can be shown that an anlysis of 'worthwhile' in terms of pleasure does not lead to consequences that do violence to common sense, that is a point in its favour.

One problem for utilitarianism has always been that its implications are misunderstood. Many reject it because they feel that acceptance of it would lead to conclusions that are incompatible with fixed beliefs to which they adhere. In some cases, no doubt, there may be such conflict (which is not to say that utilitarianism is necessarily at fault; maybe we are at fault in clinging fixedly to some of our beliefs). But it is one of my beliefs that, properly understood, utilitarianism as a matter of fact involves very little such conflict. Its great strength would appear to be precisely that it explains morality in a manner that is compatible not only with what seem to be our natural sentiments but with the hard fact of experience that we nonetheless differ from time to time on questions of value.

And so I wrote what is now Chapter 4, which is the main chapter of this book and carries the burden of the essay. It involves the outline of a specific curriculum. It is not couched in terms of high-level aims or distant objectives, but proceeds by explaining the nature of particular pursuits and arguing for their inclusion in a common curriculum. It thus represents the natural and practical sequel to two of my more abstract books concerned with utilitarianism.[3] The connection of this curriculum with utilitarianism lies in the fact that the reasons given for the inclusion of the various pursuits and activities only make sense finally in the light of the utilitarian premiss, or so I claim.

Then I decided that what I had written could not very well be left to stand on its own: the opportunities for misunderstanding were too great. The reader would need some account of the utilitarian premiss, and so I wrote what is now Chapter 3. I did not want to get involved once again in the general ethical theory of utilitarianism, and I did not want to repeat what I have written elsewhere. I therefore confined myself to a statement of the utilitarian position, by means of a critique of MacIntyre's paper 'Against Utilitarianism',[4] and to outlining an analysis of the notion of a worthwhile activity in terms of pleasure, as a hypothesis. The final confirmation of the hypothesis is to be found, in my view, in the plausibility of the claim that the curriculum that follows from it is educationally worthwhile.

I included a consideration of J. P. White's recent treatment of the notion of an intrinsically worthwhile activity at the beginning of the chapter. White's *Towards a Compulsory Curriculum*,[5] notwithstanding my criticisms of it in the text, is, in my view, one of the most important books to have been published in this area in recent years.

I was still not entirely satisfied, since there is abundant evidence to suggest that few will take a new theory seriously, if they are already committed to an existing theory. Accordingly, in the present Chapter 2, I reviewed a number of prominent views on the construction of a worthwhile curriculum, seeking to show that none of them are entirely satisfactory.

Finally I decided that an introductory chapter was needed to explain what was going on and to make a few points about the nature of theorising about the curriculum.

The four chapters fall conveniently into two groups. Part 1 of the essay, consisting of the first two chapters, is mainly critical, whereas Part 2 is essentially positive.

As before, I have tried to produce a book that will be used as a stimulus to discussion and thought, while at the same time trying to be positive in my approach and to avoid the detached fence-sitting of much philosophy. But on this occasion my main objective is to show, by doing it rather than talking about it, just how practical the consequences of theorising may be. The reader may reject every word of my argument, if he can show that it is deficient, but what he cannot do is deny that, if the argument is valid, it leads directly to positive prescription for the curriculum.

Notes and references

1 R. Barrow, *Moral Philosophy for Education* (George Allen & Unwin, 1975), p. 156.
2 Ibid., p. 159.
3 *Moral Philosophy for Education*, op. cit., and *Plato, Utilitarianism and Education* (Routledge & Kegan Paul, 1975).
4 A. MacIntyre, 'Against Utilitarianism', in T. Hollins (ed.), *Aims in Education: The Philosophic Approach* (University of Manchester, 1964).
5 J. P. White, *Towards a Compulsory Curriculum* (Routledge & Kegan Paul, 1973).

PART 1. CRITICAL COMMENTS ON CURRICULUM THEORY

Chapter 1

Towards a Worthwhile Curriculum

I WHO ARE THE CURRICULUM EXPERTS?

A warning shot will now be fired across the bows of that approaching juggernaut the good ship Lollipop. The good ship Lollipop does not have a captain. It is run by the crew. They are an able crew: some are skilled helmsmen, some are competent engineers, some have consider-able expertise with radar, and so on. In fact there is not a skill necessary to running the ship that is not possessed by one or more of the crew. In addition, all of them are sincerely concerned about the welfare of their passengers, and count it as part of their job to get on well with them and to make their trip a pleasant one.

Unfortunately, however, not one of the crew has the first idea of where the ship is going or, indeed, why it is going at all. They appreciate their own shortcomings in this respect, although they are somewhat contemptuous of those who would make too much of it. And they are aware that one or two passengers are over-anxious about this state of affairs and need to be reassured. Therefore, making a virtue of necessity, and taking a cue from the name of their ship, they allay unease by preaching a sophisticated version of the 'suck it and see' argument.

It is true, they acknowledge, that they did not begin the trip with a fixed idea of where they were going, still less did they have good reason for going to one place rather than another. But that is partly because there are no experts in such matters, as there are experts in radar or steering, and partly because it does not actually matter very much where the ship goes, so long as all is well from day to day and everybody enjoys and makes something of the trip. Besides, some preconceived plan would probably prove totally unrealistic and have to be altered in the face of actual conditions. Conversely a destination is bound to arise out of their day to day experiences.

One of the stewards, who asked innocently *how* they were to judge whether things were 'going well' from day to day, or whether a particular passenger was 'making something' of the trip, was thrown off at Gibraltar, where the Lollipop happened to have arrived, on the grounds that he was a pedant and an agitator. (In fairness, it must be admitted that he went further than this, asking such peculiar questions as whether enjoyment was all that mattered, and whether the destination arrived at through experience would necessarily be desirable. According to one of the stokers, he also made some odd remark to the effect that he was not sure that a 'destination' arrived at accidentally counted as a destination at all.)[1]

The warning shot is necessary because the good ship Lollipop is about to hit me.

The ship of education sails not simply without a coherent view of its destination, but with a crew some at least of whom believe that this state of affairs is positively desirable. There are straws in the wind that suggest that once again crude and artificial barriers are going to be raised between practice and theory. Let prospective teachers learn how to teach, runs the argument. What has abstract theory got to do with the practical problems of the classroom? In preparing potential teachers for their job we should be concerned, as it were, with the criteria adequate to giving someone a licence to teach. Such criteria might include the ability to get on well with children or with other adults, the ability to stimulate and the ability to make use of audio-visual aids, but they would not include an ability to indulge in abstract theorising. And so we face the prospect of being caught up in a whirlwind of technology and methodological wizardry. We are back with the notion of training teachers rather than educating them.

It is my firm belief that this tendency towards training ought to be resisted. It is based on a facile distinction between theory and practice, and prejudges the question at issue by thinking in terms of 'a licence to teach'. Why do we not think in terms of 'a licence to be a teacher'? Does not that shift of terminology give rise to certain questions? Would we regard somebody as suitable to being a teacher who had never thought about wider educational issues, such as the arguments for and against comprehensive schools, whether children ought to be taught what they are being taught, and whether a good case can be made for leaving children to decide for themselves what they wish to learn? I would think not, and intelligent consideration of such questions would demand a certain amount of competent theorising.

There is a very real danger that the split between practising teachers on the one hand and educational theorists on the other will come to resemble that between the Anglo-Indians and the representatives of government in England itself during the latter years of the nineteenth century. Anglo-Indians would curse members of parliament 'as "globe trotters"', and insist pathetically, like all entrenched colonials, that only they, the men on the spot, knew what things were really like, and what policies were really necessary'.[2] The result of this attitude was a steady and remarkably successful opposition to various viceroys, appointed by the home government, 'who tried to govern the sub-continent with some regard to liberal principles and little regard for illiberal prejudices'.[3] For the truth is that 'being on the spot and know-ing the native' is neither necessary nor sufficient, although no doubt it is generally one important asset, for determining wisely how affairs ought to be conducted. It is a sad trend that would turn teachers into colonials.

However I do not need to pursue the specific question of teacher education here. For whatever we think appropriate in the way of a course for potential teachers, presumably nobody can deny that there is still room for some people to be concerned with the serious study of education. That is to say there are many many questions, of which 'Is there a good case for concluding that children ought to study certain specified things?' is but one, which are patently meaningful and im-portant. Whether we conclude that it would be desirable for practising teachers to think about such a question or not, it is undeniable that it is a question worth trying to answer.

Education is not a game and children's lives are not to be lightly played with. It is intolerable that a great deal of educational practice should be the outcome of the whims of individuals (be they local government officers, headmasters or teachers) who have not even thought about, much less understood, most of the serious research and argument relevant to the question of what should go on in schools. It is an outrage on our children, as well as an offence to reason, that band-wagons of educational gimmickry, preceded by resounding and vacuous slogans, should career over and crush them, determining and limiting their future, for no better reason than that we are unwilling to pause and do some slow and painstaking thinking. Like children our-selves we are seduced by the glitter and glamour of a new idea, without the patience to examine its real worth. We emote loosely about the desirability of developing critical minds, questioning attitudes, and problem-solving capacities in children, while conspicuously failing to exhibit these qualities in our own reflections on education.

We need, ideally, to inform ourselves of and to understand all the ideas, arguments and evidence that have ever been put forward in rela-tion to the upbringing of children. We need, in practice and in par-ticular, to address ourselves to a detailed examination of the various ideas that are currently being championed, on what should be taught and how it may most effectively be taught, if we are to be entitled to claim that we did our best to consider the interests of our children rather than fulfil our prejudices. This essay is concerned primarily with the former question ('What should be taught?'). It is concerned with trying to outline and argue for a specific curriculum.

Some, out of patience with my indignation and my clear intention to indulge in yet more theorising, may laconically observe that curriculum theory is already a growth industry. There are already a great many curriculum experts around. Indeed, nominally, there are. But of whom or of what does this strange and expanding breed of curriculum experts actually consist? Who are these people whose expertise is apparently in designing curricula, as yours or mine might be in teaching mathematics or philosophising?

What after all is the curriculum? In its broadest sense it is synonymous with the content of education. Etymologically it is the course to be run. Generalising grossly, and confining ourselves for the moment to the secondary school, we have been familiar with the notion of essentially two types of curriculum for a long time now. One, the typical grammar school curriculum, designed for the more 'academic', consists of certain subjects which in the minds of many are hallowed by tradition: subjects such as maths, modern languages, classics and English, although it is worth noting that English, for example, only received the status of a respectable study at university level at the turn of the century. In addition grammar schools have been concerned with certain other subjects, sometimes regarded as being of rather doubtful pedigree, such as geography, biology, sociology, and economics.

At the other extreme has been the 'non-academic' technical or vocational curriculum consisting of activities such as woodwork and metalwork, and often geared to other more or less demanding types of apprenticeship. For a vast number of children the reality has lain between these two extremes in a watered-down version of the grammar school curriculum.

The extent to which this stereotyped tripartite picture ever was, or still remains, a faithful account of the actual situation is not our immediate concern. What is important to note is that those who are concerned to redesign the curriculum may attack this pattern from a number of different angles so that many curricula proposals scarcely resemble any part of the stereotype, even in form.

It is not simply that traditional subjects have been challenged and had their presumed value questioned, although that has happened, as in the surge away from classics. It is not simply that new subjects are proposed for inclusion in the school curriculum, although that too happens (psychology being the most recent example). It is not even simply that the whole notion of 'subjects' has sometimes come under fire, although that has also happened so that advocates of the topic approach, areas of study and the integrated curriculum exist in no short supply. More than this, in some proposals curriculum comes to include fieldwork, games, outward bound courses, visits abroad or sex education; in others the distinction between curricular and what used to be termed extra-curricular activities, such as chess clubs or debating societies, disappears; proposals for an integrated day sometimes eradicate a distinction between lessons and break; a recent book on the curriculum defined it as 'all the experiences for learning which are planned and organised by the school'.[4] and some proposals even define curriculum in terms of *how* the child learns whatever he learns, rather than in terms of *what* he learns.

And why not? But once we appreciate the nature and the variety of ways in which planning a curriculum may proceed, it surely becomes apparent that designing a curriculum is virtually equivalent to defining education itself. To propose a specific curriculum, when the term curriculum is so vague and all-embracing, is effectively to put forward a view of what education ought to consist of or of what education really is. From which it follows that to be an expert on curriculum is – or rather ought to be – to be an expert on education.

Now, despite the fact that there are many who are nominally lecturers in education, it is doubtful whether there are more than a few who could lay claim to the degree of expertise in education that the majority of lecturers in, say, physics or German could claim in their field. For what is absolutely certain is that education is not a single discipline or a unique form of knowledge : it is a field of enquiry or an area of study in which a number of different kinds of question and problem arise, often in relation to one single issue. To make a reasonable claim to competence in this sphere one would need to give evidence, at least, of one's expertise in child psychology, sociology and philosophy. In addition I should have thought that we would rightly be wary of one who had expertise in these disciplines, but who revealed himself to be ignorant of the history of education, and in particular of the ways in which various changes in education seem in fact to have come about, one who was unfamiliar with precisely what is involved in the various subjects or areas of study that might be proposed as educationally desirable, or one who was unaware of the myriad activities that are going on in different schools, and lacking in first-hand experience of such activities. The truth is that most of us who are misleadingly called lecturers in education are in fact, at best, specialists in some discipline or field that has a contribution to make to the sphere of education, but which cannot in itself finally resolve any specific educational issue.

Similarly the question 'How should we redesign the curriculum?' is clearly not a question like 'How may we most effectively get children to speak French?' nor like the question 'Is it worthwhile getting children to speak French?' nor like 'Is it economically advisable to get children to speak French, now that we are members of the Common Market?' nor like 'Does Latin effectively develop logical minds?' nor like 'Is English literature a relevant form of study?' nor like 'Can one educate the emotions through dance?' It involves having answers to all these questions – some of which are of logically distinct kinds and need to be approached in quite different ways – and to a thousand more as well.

Whether many of those who appear to be specialists in the field of curriculum are in fact competent in the various disciplines that would be required to examine these different kinds of question is not for me to say. But I think that it is now sufficiently clear that an expert in education or in curriculum, given the all-embracing nature that the term is now seen to have, if such there be, would be a formidable individual. The mass of us must surely be content to make our specific and limited contribution to the resolution of such questions as 'What should the curriculum consist of?'

II PHILOSOPHY AND THE CURRICULUM

That is one side of the coin: that the study of education involves a variety of disciplines and that no single discipline can in itself resolve any substantial complex educational issue. The other side is that we must stand out firmly for the notion that those questions and problems which arise in relation to educational issues that logically belong to a specific discipline must be answered or examined by those who have competence in the discipline in question. To be specific, we must insist that those questions and problems that arise in the context of curriculum planning which are philosophical in kind should be examined by those who are philosophically competent. Only a fool would seek answers to medical questions from those who had not studied medicine; similarly, only a fool would seek answers to philosophical questions from those who had not studied philosophy.

What sort of questions and problems are philosophical, then? What is the nature of the philosopher's contribution to the curriculum? It is varied. There are many philosophical questions to be raised, particularly when it comes to examining the arguments for various specific curricular proposals. For one of the concerns of philosophy is with clarity and coherence of argument, with specific reference to the precise meaning of concepts which, if left unexamined, serve to obscure argument or, perhaps, carry it unwarrantably as a result of their emotive overtones. A catalogue of such concepts, which function rather as jokers do in a game of cards, representing whatever the player wants them to represent, would certainly include the following: 'natural', 'undynamic', 'creative', 'alienated', 'ideological', 'relevant' and 'intelligent'. Another philosophical issue that is likely to arise in relation to the curriculum is the nature of knowledge. But there is, I shall argue, one pre-eminent question that anybody who intended to plan a curriculum would need to face and which is, or rapidly becomes, a philosophical question. Namely: 'What is worthwhile?'

Why cannot this question be avoided? Some, following R. S. Peters, might argue that the concept of education itself is such that to 'educate' someone logically involves initiating that person into worthwhile activities by means that are morally acceptable.[5] There are perhaps certain problems in this view. But we can avoid becoming involved in the argument surrounding Peters' claim – which is based on his assertion that the term, at least in its central uses, is normative (i.e. that it carries with it the force of commendation as terms such as 'brave', 'good' or 'kind' do) – for clearly what *we as a matter of fact* are concerned with is a worthwhile education. And a worthwhile education must have a worthwhile curriculum or content.

This last point needs to be stressed and explained, for it may seem that I am now going back on my admission that, whereas curriculum used to be conceived of as a body of allegedly worthwhile subjects, it is now sometimes conceived of without any reference to specific activities or subjects. But it is a mistake to assume that any education or curriculum can be literally devoid of content, and this must apply even to the curriculum proposals of those who are committed to the most extreme form of *laissez-faire*. Such a person might indeed argue that children should do whatever they choose to do, and that they are being educated provided that they are given the freedom to choose. But there is still a content to this educational proposal, albeit it is a vague and wide content, for there is a principle of selection: the principle that the activities pursued by children should be those chosen by children leads to a content of education that is theoretically specifiable and limited in exactly the same kind of way as the content of the traditional grammar school curriculum. And presumably the advocate of such an approach would wish to argue that there is something worthwhile about an education the content of which is decided solely by reference to the child's choice. (I shall not pursue here the question of how meaningful it is to speak of 'choice' in relation to young children. But see Chapter 2.)

In short any proposal for a specific curriculum, even if it be for a curriculum based solely on the choice of the children in question, involves some principle (or principles) for selection or for determining what goes on. And if the proposed curriculum is put before us as an ideal, or something that we are recommended to adopt, it is clear that the proposer must be committed to the view that the content he advocates, whether it be a specific list of pursuits or an unspecified list to be determined by some principle such as pupil choice, is worthwhile. And, as Whitfield observes, 'unless we in the education service can *in some measure* be clear about our values, which are the ultimate source for our curricular intentions, the public is hardly justified in giving over a large proportion of its resources to keep us in business'.[6]

But why is the question 'What is worthwhile?' a philosophical question? As it stands the question is in fact ambiguous, for it might mean 'What activities or pursuits are worthwhile?' or it might mean 'What constitutes worthwhileness? What makes an activity worthwhile?'[7] In the former sense, when it amounts to a request for examples of worthwhile activities, the question is not specifically philosophical. No special competence, no philosophical expertise, is needed to offer one's view of what activities are worthwhile. But then such a list of examples, representing the speaker's preferred opinion, is not a great deal of use, particularly when any two people may have widely divergent views. Ideally we need to be able to assess such rival claims, and to examine whether any particular list of examples does indeed consist of activities that are worthwhile. But to do that it is obvious that we should first of all have to be clear about the concept of worthwhileness itself: we should need to know what constitutes worthwhileness, or in virtue of what an activity may legitimately be described as worthwhile. And it is this question that is philosophical in kind.

My argument is, then, that any approach to the curriculum will involve some view of what is more or less worthwhile, and that we cannot be in any position to assess that view of what things or activities are worthwhile (and hence to assess the curriculum in question), if we have not first examined the philosophical question of what constitutes worthwhileness.

But some important cautions must be added. The first is that the fact that this is a philosophical question should not be taken to imply that there is a simple answer on which all competent philosophers will agree. Philosophy, more than most disciplines, is faced with questions that, as a matter of historical fact, have received different, not to say incompatible, answers from different philosophers.

Secondly there are some philosophers who will already be suspicious of my approach, on the grounds that in asking 'What constitutes worthwhileness?' I appear to hold the view that there is some 'essential nature' to the concept of the worthwhile. I am committing myself, it might be said, to the Platonic view that there is some fixed and eternal essence to all such concepts as justice, worthwhileness or beauty. According to this criticism, the Platonic view is fundamentally misconceived : there are no 'essences', no 'forms' as Plato puts it; there are only words and the way in which people use them.[8]

But such suspicion is unnecessary. I am not necessarily thinking in Platonic terms. (I am not even sure precisely what terms Plato was thinking in.) All I wish to commit myself and the reader to at this stage is the claim that some reflection on the notion of 'worthwhile', with a view to determining what, if anything, can be said about it, is a necessary preliminary to any coherent judgement as to whether some specific activity is or is not worthwhile. We must have a clear idea of what we think is going on when we claim that something is worthwhile. It makes a material difference when we consider a specific suggestion, such as that the study of science is worthwhile, whether we are working on the assumption that to be 'worthwhile' a pursuit must necessarily have certain features.

Thirdly and most importantly – although, when the time comes, I shall suggest that things can only be worthwhile on certain conditions – it should not be assumed that my object is to establish incontrovertibly that the curriculum I outline is worthwhile. Whatever else we may say about 'worthwhile', it is clear that a proposition asserting that something is worthwhile is a value judgement. Whatever else we may say about philosophy, it is clear that over the centuries it has established that the truth of ultimate value judgements cannot realistically be said to be incontrovertibly demonstrable.

Here too it is necessary to pause and to stress precisely what is being admitted and what is not. First, I am talking only about ultimate value judgements. By an ultimate value judgement I mean a judgement that attributes intrinsic value to something or claims that something is valuable or worthwhile in itself. This is to be contrasted with judgements about extrinsic value, by which I mean claims that something is valuable as a means to some further end. It is clear that the problems that arise in relation to judgements of extrinsic value are largely empirical : whether A does have extrinsic value as a means to B depends at least partly upon whether it *is* a means to B. For most of the remainder of this essay I shall be concerned with problems relating to the notion of intrinsic value.

Secondly, to say that we are not in a position to assert the unquestionable truth of a proposition is not to say that it is necessarily untrue. For example, it is not legitimate to claim that various basic psychological axioms are incontrovertibly and demonstrably true, but it does not follow that they are not true. With many propositions the problem is simply that we lack the evidence to establish truth or false-hood: thus, it is not unquestionably true that there is no human life on any other planet. It may be true, but although we know what sort of evidence would count to settle the matter, we do not in fact have access to it all. But with some propositions the problem is rather one of deciding what kind of evidence would count. If somebody claims, for instance, that man does not have free will and that every aspect of human life is determined, it is not likely that he and those who reject his view will disagree to any marked extent on the facts of the matter. They will disagree on how to interpret the facts. The determinist will interpret certain points as evidence for his view, while the opponent of determinism will tend to reject the suggestion that they constitute evidence of any significance. Judgements of intrinsic value come into this latter category. To say that they are not unquestionably true or incontrovertibly established is to say that there is disagreement about what sort of evidence would count to validate such judgements. It is not to say that any such judgement is necessarily false.

This distinction between an unprovable proposition (one which we do not know how to prove or disprove, but which may be true or false) and a false proposition is very important, and will crop up again in the course of this essay. For the moment I merely want to draw attention to the consequence that I cannot hope to prove that certain activities are intrinsically worthwhile, if we take 'prove' to mean 'establish as incontrovertibly and demonstrably true'. I therefore do not hope to do any such thing. But what I can do is to make my reasons for regarding something as worthwhile very clear and precise, indicating exactly what I mean by calling it worthwhile, and seek to bring the reader to agree with my account.

A parallel situation arises in relation to an ideology such as Marxism or Christianity. Both these systems of belief are based upon certain fundamental axioms which are in fact unprovable propositions. 'God exists' and 'Economic factors are invariably the basic factors in social change' are not simply unproven postulates. It is difficult to see how either of them could conceivably be proven (or disproven) beyond a shadow of reasonable doubt. What is evidence to a Christian or a Marxist is not evidence to a non-Christian or a non-Marxist. But it does not follow that either proposition is necessarily false, and, more to the immediate point, it does not follow that there cannot be more and less reasonable attempts to argue for the plausibility of either thesis. In such situations providing reasons to cause the mind to assent to the truth of a proposition must serve as proof, for, by definition, there is nothing else that can.[9] And there is all the difference in the world between committing oneself to Christianity or Marxism after minute examination of the possible meanings of the claims involved, the various arguments that have been put forward for or against them, and the reasons that might incline one to accept or reject them, and doing so, without facing up to the problems involved.

I shall be content, therefore, if I can convince the reader by reasoning that my curriculum is based upon a view of the nature of the worthwhile that is relatively plausible, which is to say more plausible than alternatives. My concern is with what it is reasonable to regard as true in this sphere. My hope is to cause the reader's mind to assent to the truth of the view I put forward, which, provided it comes about as a result of understanding rather than indoctrination or intimidation, is surely proof enough.

III   CULTURAL DETERMINISM

It should by now be clear that I am engaged in the task of attempting to reason towards a worthwhile curriculum. But, some will say, such a task is misconceived from the outset, because the curriculum is culturally determined. 'If an observer looks at the curriculum of the school in any society, he will find, either stated or implied, a set of educational objectives, a body of subject matter, a list of exercises or activities to be performed, and a way of determining whether or not the objectives have been reached by the students . . . These things comprising the curriculum *are always, in every society, derived from the culture.*'[10] (My italics.) Bourdieu argues that 'in any society . . . one will find a hierarchy of "cultural legitimacy" institutionalised in the academic system, in terms of which claims for recognition are made and cultural values defined'.[11] In other words the values enshrined in the curriculum stem from the values of society at large, which are determined by the relative power of various groups. Put simply the claim may be as Hooper puts it : 'The curriculum is socially and historically located, and culturally determined. Curriculum does not develop in a vacuum but proceeds on the basis of beliefs . . . about how people learn, what human beings should be like, what society is.'[12]

That the curriculum is (in some sense) culturally determined I do not for one minute dispute. Nor do I see any necessity to quarrel with the quotations given. But it seems advisable to clarify this issue, and to make it quite clear that there is no conflict or incompatibility between those sociological observations and the task with which I am concerned, in view of a peculiar theory, currently *à la mode*,[13] according to which all truth and knowledge, indeed all phenomena up to and including the course of the planets in their revolutions, are socially determined. What such extravagant nonsense is supposed to mean is not entirely clear, and it is more than likely that some of the wilder interpretations of this kind of theory were not actually intended by those who originally propagated it. But the ground had better be cleared.

The claim that the curriculum is culturally determined is presumably meant to be a statement of fact, based on observation. Curricula can be seen to vary from culture to culture in the light of different ways of life, priorities, beliefs and so on. This I am sure is true. And no doubt it is also always likely to be true, particularly in any quasi-democratic form of society: the sort of curriculum that a people wants will naturally tend to reflect their values and their practice. All this is straightforward and rather trivial.

But of course it does not follow that a curriculum always and necessarily will be determined by the culture of the society in which it is to be found. It is perfectly conceivable that in a particular society a curriculum that is actually alien to the culture should be imposed from without. And it certainly does not follow that we, as curriculum planners, are puppets in the control of some cultural determining force. That is to say that, although we would expect a curriculum in this culture to reflect something of that culture, there is nothing to stop us reasoning beyond the here and now, and arguing that certain aspects of our culture are objectionable and that our curriculum should not reflect them.

It is at this point that the peculiar theory to which I have referred comes into play. For it seems that some wish to suggest that one cannot meaningfully escape one's cultural situation: certainly we can challenge conventionally accepted preferences and so on, but fundamentally truth and knowledge are themselves socially and culturally determined. Now what on earth does this mean? I am not altogether sure. But of one thing I am sure, which is all that is necessary to the present purpose: it cannot mean anything that leads to the conclusion that there is in the nature of things no such thing as objective truth or knowledge. It cannot mean anything that leads to a conclusion such as 'The truth is as you see it'. Alternatively, if it does mean anything that leads to such a conclusion, then the thesis is plainly false.

There are three things that the thesis might fairly obviously mean. First, that a number of propositions that we take to be true, are true only because of specific cultural and social conditions. And to this it may be added that we are sometimes blinkered in our perception of possibilities by our cultural situation. Secondly, it may be suggested that the truth of propositions is determined by the meaning of the words employed in them and that words acquire meaning through a cultural environment. Thirdly, it might be claimed that a society creates truth by its expectations, which are revealed through its language.

A single example will help to illustrate all three of these claims. It might be suggested that the notion, and hence the problem, of delinquent children is a culturally determined phenomenon. The first point would be the simple observation that social conditions may lead to delinquency. No problem here, except to stress that it could hardly be said to be proved beyond all reasonable doubt that delinquency is solely the product of a particular range of environments. The second point would be that the observation that we have some delinquent children is only true because of what we mean by 'delinquent'. Well, it is not only true because of this : its truth is also dependent on there being children of a certain sort. But, yes, it must be conceded that it would cease to be true if we changed the meaning of 'delinquent' to 'people with wings'. So what? This cannot be taken to involve the conclusion that it is language that creates phenomena. It is through language that we are enabled to classify and categorise phenomena, certainly. But categorising people as 'delinquent' clearly has nothing to do with creating behaviour of the sort that we now happen to describe as delinquent. At least it does not, except in so far as the third point is valid.

The third point would be that by recognising a category of behaviour that we call 'delinquency' we cause delinquency. There may well be some truth in this suggestion. That is to say it is possible that by labelling a child as 'delinquent' we both behave towards him in a certain way that encourages delinquency on his part and misjudge some of his actions in the light of our prior expectations. More generally it is also possible that a general recognition of something called 'delinquency', leading to much talk and study on the subject, puts ideas into people's heads.

So much may be granted. But there is nothing here that establishes either that the proposition 'We have some delinquent children' is not an objective matter of fact, or that no individuals would behave in ways that we happen to label delinquent, if we did not think of them as such.

The truth is that the truth is not as you see it. The truth is as it is, because what we mean by a true proposition is a proposition that states what is the case, rather than what someone happens to take to be the case. Nor is there in principle any problem about knowledge, if we assume that to know something involves (1) that the something in question is true, (2) that one believes it to be true and (3) that one has evidence for its truth. Where there is of course a problem, at a deep level, is over the question of how we can ever know for certain that we know something, since this would require having evidence that the evidence one has for the truth of a proposition is adequate. But on a commonsense level this is not generally a problem of great severity. It is true that I am now writing this page, I know that it is true, and only a madman or a philosopher could seriously doubt it.[14]

My conclusion is that, though no doubt sense can be made of the claim that truth and knowledge are culturally determined, there is no reason to accept any interpretation of that proposition which implies that there is no such thing as a fact which can be known to be the case or an argument which can be seen to be valid, independently of cultural considerations, or which suggests that we are inescapably determined with respect to our perceptions and judgements by our cultural background. Consequently, although it may well be true that current curriculum practice has been predominantly culturally determined, not a great deal follows from this observation with reference to our immediate concern.

Explanation is not the same as justification. Even if the existence of specific curricular practice is correctly to be explained in terms of cultural causes, this has no bearing on the question of justification for such practice. Since our concern is with the search for a curriculum which we can produce good reason to regard as worthwhile,[15] we can proceed without reference to or fear of the suggestion that the curriculum is culturally determined.

IV INTEGRATION

One final issue needs to be raised here and that is the matter of integration. The basic problem with discussing 'integration' is that people mean different things by it. Some use the term 'integrated' to denote a programme that seeks to relate the independent study of various disciplines. Others see an integrated course in terms of theme-teaching. Both those approaches are obviously to be distinguished from yet a third sense of integrated studies such as the Inter-Disciplinary Enquiry approach promulgated by the Goldsmiths' College Curriculum Laboratory. The IDE, as it is called, demands 'a completely unstructured approach . . . one in which the subjects as such do not make an appearance at all'.[16]

A second problem involved in discussing integrated curricula is that it is not always clear whether various teaching methods are seen as necessarily linked to the course in question, or merely as desirable ways of teaching, which might be employed both in relation to an integrated curriculum and various non-integrated curricula. For example, the IDE approach is closely linked in practice with the idea of 'learning by discovery'. But it is not entirely clear whether the claim is that true learning by discovery can only take place in the sort of teaching situation envisaged, or whether 'learning by discovery' is merely one feature of this approach, which it might well share with other curricula programmes. The claim that 'Enquiry, research and discovery . . . are the methods of approach almost universally adopted by Integrated Studies'[17] is similarly ambiguous. Does this imply that some kind of integrated approach is *necessary*, if enquiry, research and discovery are to be used as methods of approach? Or merely that as a matter of fact advocates of integration happen to be amongst those who would advocate such methods?

These two problems lead to a third major problem: namely the difficulty of sorting out different kinds of argument for integrated studies, in order to try and assess them. There is a considerable difference, for instance, between a motivational argument for a programme of related studies, and an epistemological argument for a theme-centred approach. It is one thing to claim that children will be more interested if their subject studies are related, another to claim that the nature of knowledge is such that subject divisions impose artificial barriers.

I do not intend to review all the different kinds of argument that might be produced in favour of different kinds of integrated programme. I confess to finding all variants of what Pring has called the 'strong thesis' for curriculum integration, namely some view to the effect that knowledge is a seamless whole, unsatisfactory.[18] All claims as to the unity of all knowledge with which I am familiar seem to turn out, on closer examination, to be incomprehensible, trivial or plain false. I cannot, in other words, see warrant for any view of the nature of knowledge that involves the conclusion that true knowledge must necessarily be better acquired through some form of integrated studies.

I do not dispute the possible truth of the empirical observation that real-life problems are often complex affairs involving many dimensions and that teaching different subjects as totally distinct entities may militate against developing a comprehensive and multi-dimensional perspective in children. For example teaching history as history, literature as literature, and so on, may tend to militate against the likelihood of an individual relating aspects of these subjects or seeing in specific situations an historical, literary or other dimension. But it should be stressed that this kind of claim is empirical (rather than anything to do with the nature of knowledge as such), is not in fact backed by any particularly strong evidence, and is in danger of obscuring one of the points that is actually involved in it: namely that the historical, literary or other dimensions to any given situation are in some way distinct and that this needs to be appreciated, if the individual wishes to avoid making a complete fool of himself.

Nor do I find the claim that integrated programmes promote 'enquiring, critical minds capable of research and sound judgement' very persuasive.[19] To know whether this were true, we should first of all need to have a rather more systematic account of what is meant by such phrases as 'a critical mind' and 'sound judgement' than we are usually given. But we should also need some empirical evidence resulting from research carried out in the light of that clear explication of the meaning of the objectives.

In the meantime, given the lack of any such decisive evidence, it should be stressed that from the fact that a learning situation involves the need for, say, individual research, it does not automatically follow that such a situation is either necessary or sufficient to produce an able researcher, nor that it is the best way to seek to do so. This important point can be generalised: providing children with opportunities to be, do or exercise A is not necessarily the best way of helping them to be, do well or exercise capably A, as adults. For example, granting children autonomy is not necessarily the best way of developing truly autonomous adults.[20] A 'critical mind capable of research and sound judgement' fairly obviously involves more than mere willingness to enquire into something. It requires, presumably, competence and knowledge in various spheres. It might be the case – I don't say that it is, but that it might be – that some integrated programmes, though they provided opportunities for enquiry and research, failed to develop such competence and knowledge. Or it might be the case that an enquiring attitude could as well be developed as the culmination of a learning situation which was not primarily concerned with providing opportunities for exercising it.

However, I do not wish to be taken to be opposing all forms of integrated curricula. I am not here concerning myself with arguments for and against specific programmes of integration because, as already stated, in what follows I am primarily concerned with the question of what the content of the curriculum should be, and not with the question of how to arrange that content or how to present it for teaching purposes. An integrated curriculum has to integrate something, and I am interested in the prior question of what that something should be.

The reason that I raise the question of integration at all is simply this: in most of what follows, particularly in the final chapter, I shall proceed by reference to various separate items and I shall treat them individually. Thus I shall deal with science, history and literature as distinct entities. I do this for the excellent reason that one thing I shall be concerned to examine is what is distinctive about these pursuits; for one thing is manifest and that is that *some* kind of distinctions can be drawn between such pursuits. But the fact that I proceed in that manner should not be taken to suggest that I am necessarily proposing that they should be taught as distinct elements in watertight compartments. Whether there is a case for integrating the various elements that I argue to be necessary to a worthwhile curriculum is a separate question, and one which I do not intend to try to answer.

V CONCLUSION

'Towards' is a useful word that provides one with an excuse for failing to get where one claims to be going. What I have tried to suggest in this chapter is that it is right and proper to use it in reference to the curriculum. A philosopher, writing as a philosopher, can only go so far. But what he can and should do is face up to the paramount question of the nature of the worthwhile. The fact that a teacher can be a very good teacher without ever having given consideration to such a question must not blind us to the fact that the question is there. Some answer to it is necessarily presupposed in judging a teacher to be good, for presumably what we mean by describing him as a good teacher is that he effectively succeeds in some worthwhile enterprise.

In addition, I have argued, by way of preliminaries, that: (1) the fact that we cannot demonstrate incontrovertibly that a particular curriculum is worthwhile is not sufficient reason to conclude that it is pointless to examine the question – we may still find good reason to regard one curriculum as preferable to another; (2) that some thought on the concept of worthwhileness itself is a necessary preliminary to attempting to assess the relative value of competing curricula; (3) that this emphasis on reason and what we may hope to achieve by it, is not discredited by sociological observations to the effect that the curriculum is culturally determined and (4) that to examine various activities or pursuits as independent entities should not be construed as necessarily a rejection of integrated curricula.

With these points made, I shall now proceed to look critically at a wide variety of alternative approaches to the construction of a worthwhile curriculum.

Notes and references

1 This analogy owes something to Plato, *Republic*, 488.A.
2 M. Fido, *Rudyard Kipling* (Hamlyn, 1974), p. 34.
3 Ibid., p. 34.
4 R. C. Whitfield (ed.), *Disciplines of the Curriculum* (McGraw Hill, 1971), p. 2.

5   R. S. Peters, *Ethics and Education* (George Allen & Unwin, 1966), pt. 1. Peters's work on the concept of education is surely too well known to require further comment here. I have cited an early statement of his position, despite the fact that he has since modified it, because it remains one of the fullest. At scattered intervals below I shall indicate certain misgivings that I have about the nature of Peters' exercise.

6   R. C. Whitfield, op. cit., p. 4.

7   I have been told more than once that the word 'worthwhileness' does not exist. It does now. Language grows and develops. I have coined this noun because it is needed.

8   Those unfamiliar with Plato's theory of ideas (or forms) who are interested in finding out more about it may care to look at: Plato, *Euthyphro*, *Republic* (esp. 471–543), and G. C. Field, *The Philosophy of Plato* (Oxford, 1969), chs 1, 2.

9   The substitution of 'reasons that may cause the mind to assent' for 'proof' derives from J. S. Mill. See J. S. Mill, *Utilitarianism* (Fontana, 1962), ch. 2; R. Barrow, *Plato, Utilitarianism and Education* (Routledge & Kegan Paul, 1975), ch. 5, and *Moral Philosophy for Education* (George Allen & Unwin, 1975), ch. 3.

10 B. O. Smith, W. O. Stanley and J. H. Shores, 'Fundamentals of Curriculum Development', in R. Hooper (ed.), *The Curriculum: Context, Design and Development* (Oliver & Boyd, 1971).

11 P. Bordieu, 'Intellectual Field and Creative Project', in M. F. D. Young (ed.), *Knowledge and Control* (Collier–Macmillan, 1971). The quotation is from Young's introduction (p. 11) summarising Bourdieu.

12 R. Hooper, op. cit., Introduction, p. 2.

13 Versions of some such theory are prevalent amongst my students, but I am thinking primarily of contributors to M. F. D. Young, op. cit., such as Esland, Blum and Keddie. Only space prevents me from offering a full critique of that volume here. But, on a similar theme, see below, ch. 2.vi.

14 My account of 'truth' and 'knowledge', though not beyond dispute, is fairly standard. For an introductory but considerably fuller account of such a view, see J. Hospers, *An Introduction to Philosophical Analysis* (Routledge & Kegan Paul, 1956), ch. 2.

15 May not that good reason which we might produce itself be culturally determined? I have relegated this question to a footnote since the argument might go on *ad infinitum*. My reply would be: What we are prepared to count as a 'good reason' may indeed be 'culturally determined' in one of the ways distinguished in the text. What I do not accept is that whether something does constitute a 'good reason' must *necessarily* be merely a matter of cultural determinates. Thus wanting to be a bus driver provides a good reason for learning to drive in a way that other things may not. Certainly the example of driving only makes sense in certain cultural settings, but the fact that wanting to be a bus driver constitutes a good reason for learning to drive does not depend in any way upon cultural conditions. It just is one possible good reason.

16 D. Warwick (ed.), *Integrated Studies in the Secondary School* (University of London Press, 1973), p. 2.

17 Ibid., p. 10.

18 R. Pring, 'Curriculum Integration', in R. S. Peters (ed.), *The Philosophy of Education* (Oxford, 1973).

19 This claim is put forward by D. Warwick, op. cit., pp. 9–10. It is perhaps slightly more plausible than his suggestion that integrated studies 'will more

than have succeeded' if they do no more than force us to ask ourselves such questions as whether they are a good idea (p. 6).

20   As Dearden has pointed out. R. F. Dearden, 'Autonomy and Education', in R. F. Dearden, P. H. Hirst and R. S. Peters (eds), *Education and the Development of Reason* (Routledge & Kegan Paul, 1972).

Chapter 2

Alternative Approaches to the Curriculum

Many educationalists do not choose to examine the question of what, if anything, is worthwhile and why it is so. They prefer either simply to assert their own values or to accept a consensus of opinion on worthwhile aims and to formulate their educational objectives in the light of those unquestioned aims. But, since any curricular proposals that are put forward as desirable proposals logically involve a view of what is worthwhile, no one who deals in curricular recommendations can avoid committing himself, by implication at least, to a specific view about what is worthwhile. If we search hard enough, any curriculum proposals will be found to depend upon a particular conception of what is worthwhile – a bone, so to speak, perhaps obscured by the flesh of the theory in question, but nonetheless there.

There are at least two good reasons for devoting some time to the consideration of other people's views as to what constitutes a worthwhile curriculum or to the examination of the bones of various curriculum theories. First, if we accept as a premiss that the question of what constitutes a worthwhile curriculum is decidedly complex and perhaps does not admit of a simple categorical answer, then, in order to arrive at anything that we might reasonably call a well-founded opinion, we surely ought to be aware of and examine seriously alternative opinions. Curriculum theory is, after all, in the last analysis concerned with the very practical question of what children do in schools. It is a fact, which we would do well to recognise and take seriously, that different people have put forward arguments, which they at least think compelling, for very different kinds of curricula. There is surely an important difference between holding to a particular opinion about what the curriculum should consist of, when one has examined, understood and found wanting rival theories, and holding to that same opinion in ignorance of alternatives.

Secondly, in putting forward one's own view of what constitutes a worthwhile curriculum, as I shall do in this essay, one obviously thereby rejects other accounts. One way, therefore, of reasoning towards the acceptance of one's own view is to attempt to indicate the shortcomings in other approaches. This is a particularly appropriate procedure in a matter such as this where relative plausibility rather than conclusive or final proof is looked for. We have to make a decision as to what children should do. We therefore have to consider the relative strength of different arguments for different conclusions. That we could scarcely do, without examining seriously alternative approaches to the curriculum.

I   PRACTICAL TEACHING OBJECTIVES AND CONTINGENT VALUES

I shall look first at Stanley Nisbet's attempt to locate reasons for teaching particular subjects in his book *Purpose in the Curriculum*.[1] He begins by outlining what he calls 'intermediate or practical objectives of education'. These, as their name suggests, are designed as objectives which the practising teacher might realistically strive to meet. They are deliberately put forward in place of higher and more general aims of education, such as 'liberating the human spirit' or facilitating 'complete living', on the grounds that these latter aims are too vague to be meaningful. What would the teacher bent on 'liberating the human spirit' actually be supposed to do from day to day?

It is worth outlining Nisbet's practical objectives in full. They fall into two groups. The first group comes under the general heading 'adjustment to environment' and involve the cultivation of skills necessary for social life, initiation into the culture of the community, preparation for fulfilling a family role, preparation for a job, preparation for leisure and preparation for active participation in a democracy. The second group is concerned with 'personal growth' and involves concern for physical, aesthetic, social, spiritual, intellectual and moral development.

In the light of these objectives, Nisbet then proceeds to examine virtually all existing curriculum subjects, from classics to carpentry and from reading to religious instruction, in order to see what contribution each subject can make to meeting the various objectives.

On the face of it such an approach is eminently sensible, and it certainly involves attempting to produce grounds for the study of some things rather than others in schools. But a closer look reveals two extremely unsatisfactory features of this procedure, the first to do with the list of objectives and the second with what is said about the various subjects.

No argument is given for adopting the objectives listed. Nisbet is aware of this and explains that to seek to justify them as objectives would involve moving into the realm of philosophy. This he does not wish to do, since his purpose is precisely to stay in a realm that is of immediate significance to the practising teacher. His deliberate intention is to bridge the gap between theory and practice by interposing these practical objectives between 'remote, abstruse, "absolute" aims which have no influence on practice' and highly specific teaching aims such as getting through a particular exercise in a given period of time.

Perhaps this may seem a laudable intention. But the fact remains that we have been given no reason to accept these objectives. They may have the merit of being practical, but they have the demerit of being entirely arbitrary, until such time as an argument is presented to show why we should adopt them. Nor is this a purely academic matter. Many would sincerely question some of Nisbet's objectives. For example, many would object to the idea that the school should be actively concerned to promote spiritual development. And if that is so, surely we have to be prepared to discuss the merits and demerits of that objective.

Furthermore the distinction between high-level aims, which are vague and effectively meaningless, and intermediate objectives, which are not, is highly misleading. The high-level aims that Nisbet cites are certainly hopelessly vague, but that is because a phrase such as 'liberating the human spirit' is vague, not because it is high-level. One might reasonably point out that the phrases 'spiritual development' and 'moral development' are hardly less vague, even though they are classified as practical objectives.

What I am suggesting is that the distinction between high-level aims and practical objectives does not get us anywhere. A statement of aims is not necessarily unclear or vague just because it is general or high-level. What is needed at all levels is precision and clarity. We need ultimate aims that are sufficiently clear to allow us to deduce immediate teaching objectives from them, and those teaching objectives in their turn must be clear and precise. Nisbet's objectives, although many of them may happen to appeal to many of us, are nonetheless presented as mere *fiats.* Some of them are rather obscure, with the result that it is difficult to determine whether one accepts them or not. Some of them would in all probability be challenged as objectives by some people. None of them have been shown to be objectives which there is good reason to adopt.

The second unsatisfactory feature of Nisbet's approach to the curriculum can be deduced from the fact that by the end of the exercise virtually every school subject that has ever been devised is shown to be justifiable in terms of many more than one of the objectives. Commercial subjects, for example, such as typing and shorthand, are not only regarded as making a contribution to the objectives of promoting social skills and preparing the individual for a job, but are also said by

Nisbet to make a contribution to the moral and intellectual development of the individual. And science, it is argued, contributes to the aesthetic and spiritual development of the individual.

How does Nisbet come to arrive at these slightly surprising conclusions? Basically because he concentrates on drawing attention to possible contingent consequences of studying each subject. He does not claim, for instance, that the study of science *by its nature* contributes to spiritual development. Rather he argues that the teacher of science could, if he wished, take the trouble to make a contribution to the spiritual development of his pupils. This he might do by stressing 'that science and religion are not necessarily antagonistic', or science might even 'be approached in a reverent frame of mind as the study of the wonderful works of a Creator'.[2] Similarly the contribution of a typing course to moral development is said to stem from the fact that in such a course application to work, self-discipline and increased amour-propre can be developed.

This may be so, but the obvious objection to this kind of approach is that subjects appear to be being justified by considerations which in fact have nothing to do with the subjects themselves. To enter into discussion of the question of whether science and religion are necessarily antagonistic is to go well beyond studying science. Certainly a typing course might promote self-discipline, but so might stamp-collecting. Drawing attention to the possible contingent consequences of studying various subjects or engaging in various pursuits gives us no principle of selection between the many subjects competing for curriculum time, and offers no reason for necessarily studying any one of them.

Two points emerge from this brief consideration of Nisbet's approach to the curriculum. First that ideally we should like to locate some teaching objectives that, besides being clear and practical, can be convincingly argued for. Secondly that, if we wish to maintain that the curriculum should consist of some subjects rather than others, we need to make reference to features that are an integral part of the subject. If we wish to argue that children ought to study science, for example, then we need to produce reasoning to show that there is something about studying science itself that is valuable, rather than merely that one might use science as well as anything else to develop such qualities as perseverance or concern for accuracy.

Nisbet's approach involves setting up certain objectives and examining all actual curriculum subjects to see whether they might not be used to make a contribution to those objectives. That this approach is decidedly unsatisfactory can perhaps best be seen from the fact that, according to Nisbet, what he terms extra-curricular activities such as athletics, holiday camps, dances and stamp collectors' clubs contribute to every single one of his objectives. From which one concludes that there is no very compelling reason, on Nisbet's terms, to do anything other than provide opportunities for these activities. Clearly, though the point of view embodied in this conclusion (which is not, incidentally, drawn by Nisbet himself) might be championed by some, its defence would require more argument than Nisbet's approach can provide.

It is worth noting in passing that some of what has been said in reference to Nisbet applies also to the much more schematic and detailed *Taxonomy of Educational Objectives*, edited by B. S. Bloom.[3] There are, I think, a number of problems in the taxonomy itself, especially in respect of the affective domain: one might argue that some of the concepts are rather rough and ready (what actually counts as 'willingness to respond' or 'satisfaction in response'?), and consequently rather difficult to assess in practice. There is the question of whether all the various objectives put forward are particularly important, and there may be a problem in that the whole edifice is constructed on the assumption that there are generalised abilities which can be transferred across logical boundaries.

However, the point that concerns me here is that it is one thing to attempt to relate one's teaching of a particular subject to Bloom's objectives, and quite another to seek to justify teaching one's subject in the first place by reference to those objectives. Time and again one comes across attempts to justify the teaching of a specific subject which stress, no doubt correctly, that by means of the subject in question Bloom's or some similar set of objectives can be attained. But just as virtually anything could be used to subserve most of Nisbet's objectives, so virtually anything could be taught in such a way as to subserve Bloom's. One cannot therefore rely on the taxonomy in any attempt to show that biology ought to figure on the curriculum, or that time should be devoted to history rather than chemistry.

Of the many subjects or integrated programmes of one sort or another which have been championed as deserving curriculum time, I can think of few that could not be structured in such a way as to meet such objectives. But I can think of many that *prima facie* do not seem particularly worthy of inclusion in the curriculum. This impression may turn out to be unjustified. But it does at least suggest that we should look for criteria to help us distinguish between a variety of programmes in respect of worth, even though all of them may be used as means to objectives of the sort outlined by Nisbet or Bloom. Bloom's objectives in particular should be seen as encapsulating methodological rather than curricular prescriptions. Most subjects can be shown to have a value or to have some worth; the question we must surely face is the question raised by Herbert Spencer: What knowledge is of *most* worth? What is it *most* worthwhile for children to do in schools?[4]

II INTRINSIC VALUE

An alternative to trying to see whether existing curriculum subjects could be used or taught in such a way as to contribute to various pre-determined objectives is to concentrate on certain subjects, pursuits or activities themselves, and to argue that they are worthwhile in themselves. The conclusion can then be drawn that if something such as mathematics just is intrinsically worthwhile, in a way that, say, dancing is not, then schools should be concerned to initiate children into mathematics rather than into dancing.

Formally, no doubt, we shall all agree: if mathematics, or anything else, just is worthwhile, whereas dancing or whatever is not, that seems to constitute a good case for putting mathematics rather than dancing into the curriculum. If . . . But who is to say whether mathematics or anything else just is worthwhile, and how would one establish such a claim?

One answer that might be given to that question is 'by intuition'. According to this view certain pursuits are self-evidently worthwhile, others self-evidently worthless. One has to discriminate intuitively. That is all there is to it. Now of course it is conceivable that this view is correct. That is to say, it may be the case that some pursuits just are worthwhile, and that in order to show that they are we can do no more than appeal to what strikes us as their self-evident value. But if that were the case we should not have made much progress so far as constructing a curriculum goes, since people's intuitions differ radically. What you think is self-evidently worthwhile is not necessarily what I think is self-evidently worthwhile. How do we decide between your intuitive feeling that reading literature is worthwhile, mine that doing philosophy is worthwhile, and somebody else's that listening to pop music is worthwhile? Whose intuition is to count?

If it finally transpires that all we can say is that pursuits have to be assessed as worthwhile or worthless by intuition, it follows, so long as intuitive judgements as to what is worthwhile continue to differ, that we have no good grounds for insisting that any particular curriculum is worthwhile in that it consists of worthwhile pursuits. For anybody may legitimately insist that it is not worthwhile, on the grounds that he cannot see the allegedly self-evident value of the pursuits in question. If he cannot see that they are worthwhile, how can we claim that it is self-evident that they are?

One might suggest that we should treat as worthwhile those pursuits which the majority of people regard as self-evidently worthwhile. But it is not clear why we should accept this suggestion, since presumably nobody would seriously argue that the mere fact that most people think that something is worthwhile makes it so. And the consequences of accepting a majority verdict, besides ensuring a commitment to the status quo at any given time, might, from some points of view, be pretty appalling. All in all, although we have no guarantee at this stage that we can advance beyond the intuitionist view and its attendant problems, it is to be hoped that we can.

Once again it seems that what we ideally require is some reasoning related to the inherent nature of a particular activity or subject, if we wish to produce a convincing argument for that subject or activity being worthwhile in itself. A typical example of such an approach is provided by G. H. Bantock's attempt to establish the value of studying literature. His argument is that such is the nature of fine literature and poetry – complex, subtle and true to life in its portrayal of human emotions – that it must be more worthy of study, certainly than mass-produced inferior culture, and probably than a great many other different kinds of activity. 'It is not difficult to show', he writes, 'that the study of poetry involves a higher and more delicate degree of brain organisation, affects more aspects of the personality and produces more valuable consequences . . . than the study of pushpin.'[5]

I must make it clear at this point that I do not dissent from Bantock's conclusion that studying literature is a worthwhile pursuit, and that *part* of what we have to do, if we wish to put forward a reasoned defence of a particular aspect of the curriculum as worthwhile, is to consider what is necessarily involved in an activity, as he seeks to do. But for the moment I am concerned to draw attention to the problems of this kind of argument. As it stands Bantock's argument is not very satisfactory.

The phrase 'higher and more delicate degree of brain organisation' is emotive in the extreme. The implication is obviously that this type of 'brain organisation' is *better* than lower and less delicate degrees of brain organisation. Who would dare to assert that he preferred lower degrees of brain organisation? Yet there is no argument here to show that the brain organisation needed to study poetry is *better* in some general sense than that needed to do many other things, including perhaps playing pushpin. What I imagine will be widely conceded is that poetry is more complex than many other things, and that a brain that can appreciate it may *ipso facto* be said to be capable of understanding something quite complex. But there is no evidence that a brain that can appreciate poetry will necessarily be able to cope well with any other complex spheres of life. We thus do not appear to have any argument for asserting that people ought to study poetry here – only the observation that it is quite a sophisticated thing to be able to do. What is needed is some reasoning to establish the conclusion that this particular sophisticated activity is worth engaging in.

That studying poetry may have 'valuable consequences' I do not doubt, but evidently these consequences need spelling out so that we can assess them for ourselves. That it 'affects aspects of the personality' seems a rather more contentious claim, if it means more than that the study of poetry develops an awareness of poetry. What Bantock seems to mean is that the study of poetry contributes to such things as moral development and sensitivity. But, if that is the claim, it obviously needs considerable clarification and more argument.

In short there may well be something about the nature of poetry and literature in general that makes the study of it either worthwhile in itself or educationally worthwhile; and its value may lie in something to do with the features mentioned by Bantock. But the mere assertion that it is complex and produces valuable consequences, coupled with the vague claim that it affects many aspects of the personality, is hardly satisfactory. I am sure that it is a more worthwhile pursuit than pushpin, but this argument has not shown it.

R. S. Peters has attempted to show that a certain broad range of activities or pursuits, rather than particular individual activities, are worthwhile in themselves.[6] Roughly speaking his claim is that certain activities must necessarily be valued because they are by their nature concerned with the pursuit of truth. Examples of such activities would be theoretical pursuits such as the study of literature, science and history.

Peters's argument is that if anyone seriously asks a question such as 'Why put this in the curriculum rather than that?' which is merely a particular application of the general question 'Why do this rather than that?' the mere fact of his asking the question indicates that he 'must already have a serious concern for truth built into his consciousness'. He does already value the rational pursuit of truth; that much is clear from the fact that he is not content to settle the content of the curriculum arbitrarily. Consequently, since he is committed to truth and good reasoning, he cannot consistently deny value to those pursuits pre-eminently concerned with the reasoned pursuit of truth. He must value pursuits such as philosophy and science, for it is by means of them that we arrive at reasoned truth.

There is clearly something in this argument – a sincere request for some good reason for doing this rather than that does involve some kind of commitment to some degree of rationality and truth – but it will not serve to show that certain theoretical pursuits just are worth studying.

In the first place it would at best show that a certain kind of person, namely the sort of person who takes the question of curriculum content seriously, was committed to truth. It would show, if you like, that Peters and I (perhaps you) are as a matter of fact committed to some form of rationality and some concern for truth. It would not show that we are right to be so committed, or that we ought to value these things. Still less would it show that others, who do not feel inclined to pursue truth and rational justification, ought to share our values.

In the second place it does not follow from the fact that we or anyone else see the value of the rational pursuit of truth, that we or he must think it desirable that all or any particular person should engage in the rational pursuit of truth. In other words, I might quite consistently say that, when and if people ask questions such as 'Why do this rather than that?' they should be concerned for rational and true answers, but that there are more worthwhile things for people to do than ask such questions. Thirdly, all that we can safely deduce from the fact that somebody sincerely asks 'Why do this rather than that?' is that he wants a reasoned answer to *that* question. We cannot deduce that, if he is to be consistent, he must value specific pursuits such as philosophy, even if we concede that such a pursuit is concerned with the rational pursuit of truth.

Of course it would be strange to meet somebody who professed a serious interest in questions about the curriculum and more generally about what was worthwhile, and yet who appeared to see no value in pursuits such as science and philosophy. But it would be psychologically rather than logically odd. Besides which, the more important point would be that, even if he did see value in these pursuits, it would not follow that he was right to value them, and it would not follow that to be consistent he would have to conclude that all children ought to be initiated into them. Whatever else we say, therefore, we cannot conclude that Peters's argument shows that such theoretical pursuits as science and philosophy ought necessarily to figure in a worthwhile curriculum.

III FORMS OF KNOWLEDGE

P. H. Hirst attempts to ground the curriculum in the nature of knowledge itself, arguing that there are a certain number of what he calls forms of knowledge.[7] 'The domain of knowledge I take to be centrally the domain of true propositions or statements, and the question of there being logically distinct forms of knowledge to be the question of there being logically distinct types of true propositions or statements.'[8] A form of knowledge, he suggests, is distinguishable by four criteria, all of which need to be met. First, it must have certain concepts that are peculiar in character to the form, as gravity, acceleration and hydrogen are concepts peculiar in character to the form of knowledge which may be referred to as the physical sciences. Secondly, the form must have a 'distinct logical structure'. This comes about, in fact, largely as a result of the central concepts that are peculiar in character to the form. Because of the nature of a concept like 'gravity', when it functions as part of the language of the physical sciences, there is only a limited number of things that you can sensibly say employing this and other scientific concepts. Thirdly, a form, by virtue of its particular terms and logic, has expressions or statements that in some way or other are testable against experience. Finally, a form develops particular techniques and skills for exploring experience and testing its distinctive expressions.

Hirst originally claimed to discern eight forms of knowledge by these criteria: mathematics, physical sciences, human sciences, history, religion, literature and the fine arts, philosophy and moral knowledge. So the claim would appear to be that there is something which we may reasonably refer to as the physical sciences, for example, which proceeds by employing distinctive concepts that can only meaningfully be used in certain ways. When used in meaningful ways they will give rise to propositions the truth of which can be tested by distinctive means. The case is similar with the remaining forms.

Such a theory gives rise to three distinct questions: (1) Can we discern distinct forms of knowledge by Hirst's criteria? (2) If we can, what are the forms discernible? Are they the eight originally listed by Hirst, ought we to accept his later more restricted list, or are all his lists astray on his own terms? (3) Assuming that he is correct in claiming that there is a finite list of forms of knowledge, does he have a case for suggesting that ideally all children ought to be initiated into whatever forms of knowledge there are?

I shall deal with the last question first. Hirst claims that initiation into whatever forms of knowledge there are is one and the same thing as the development of the rational mind. This, I suggest, is acceptable, at least to the point of saying that such initiation is a necessary condition of the developed rational mind. It would be odd to regard an individual who could not distinguish between logically distinct types of true proposition as having a developed rational mind. But then one might reasonably ask, granted that part of what we mean by the developed rational mind is the ability to discern logically distinct types of proposition, why should we be concerned about developing rational minds and more specifically this aspect of the rational mind?

Hirst does not really have a reply to this question. He regards it as peculiar, as no doubt it is, inasmuch as few would seriously question the desirability of enabling people to distinguish between logically distinct kinds of question. There cannot be many people who would actually welcome a state of affairs in which people could not recognise the logical difference between, say, an aesthetic question and an economic question. But that is not really the point. It may seem odd to us that people should question such an objective, but some people *are* odd from our point of view. It is perfectly conceivable that somebody should sincerely question the desirability of initiating children into whatever forms there are, and therefore, ideally, we should like to be able to show why it is desirable. (Indeed, many have questioned the desirability of the sort of education that Hirst advocates, but it is not always clear whether they are questioning the principle, the practicability or the actual details of his proposals.)

Hirst's position here is very similar to that of Peters, and therefore little more needs to be said about it. He suggests that 'to ask for a justification of the pursuit of rational knowledge itself . . . presupposes some commitment to what one is seeking to justify'.[9] Only a person who was committed to the value of knowledge, of having good reasons and of truth, could seriously be concerned to ask whether there was good reason to value the development of rational mind. But the fact remains that a person might raise the question 'Why develop this aspect of the rational mind?' ('Why initiate every individual into all the forms that there are?') quite sincerely, while at the same time maintaining that he did not regard it as necessarily desirable. We may concede that it would be psychologically odd, perhaps, but it is not logically odd or inconsistent.

Brief mention should be made of R. F. Dearden's attempt to justify a similar thesis.[10] He argues that the ability to recognise whatever forms of knowledge there are is desirable since they represent 'basic constitutive elements in rational choice'. In other words, genuine individual autonomy presupposes such an ability, since ignorance and error can hamper genuine free choice as much as drunkenness or restrictions imposed by others. This is a much stronger argument, a version of which I shall make use of later. But for the moment two points should be noted: there are a number of other things, such as a mass of information and considerable experience, which are no less necessary to genuine autonomy than appreciation of whatever forms there are. Secondly, of course, Dearden's argument presupposes the value of autonomy itself, which in its turn would stand in need of justification.

I conclude that the claim that children ought to be initiated into whatever forms of knowledge there are has not, in strict logic, been satisfactorily established. Nonetheless it seems *prima facie* reasonable as a claim, and it may prove possible to argue for it more effectively. It is therefore worth going further and examining the question of the forms of knowledge themselves. Are there distinct forms, and if so what are they?

Clearly these eight things which Hirst distinguishes as forms of knowledge are distinct. They are distinct in subject matter, if nothing else. But then so are a host of other things. The question is whether they are distinct in the way that Hirst claims – whether they are distinguishable by his four criteria.

Some have found the first two criteria problematic and have wondered, for instance, what the distinctive concepts of literature are. But I do not think that we need to worry too much about that, especially as Hirst himself has subsequently suggested that it is the third criterion that is all-important.[11] The crucial question would appear to be 'How many logically distinct types of proposition, if any, can we discern?' The mark of a logically distinct type of proposition is that it is testable against experience in some unique way. If we add that Hirst has also subsequently stressed that the phrase 'testable against experience' should not be taken too literally, and that what he is really concerned about are different kinds of criteria for truth,[12] the question becomes as follows: How many distinct types of proposition are there, in the sense of types of proposition the truth of which would need to be determined by different kinds of truth criteria?

It should be noted that I have employed the phrase 'different *kinds* of truth criteria', although Hirst simply refers to 'different criteria for truth'. My reason for interfering with what he actually says is this: the phrase 'different criteria for truth' is dangerously obscure. In one sense any propositions relating to different subject matter will have 'different criteria for truth', since how you establish whether a proposition is true or false must depend to some extent on its subject matter. For example, the human sciences face problems in establishing the truth of propositions which the physical sciences do not face, because the former are not dealing with inanimate subject matter. In one sense therefore the human sciences certainly differ from the physical sciences in respect of the criteria for establishing truth. But then, looked at in this way, chemistry, biology, physics, psychology and sociology all become distinct forms of knowledge. So too do photography, astronomy, the sociology of the mass media and the philosophy of education. For each of these 'things' will give rise to propositions the truth of which will have to be assessed by criteria to some extent dependent on the subject matter. The question of whether it is true that the best way to capture the excitement of the Grand National is to photograph it in such and such a way, obviously has to be determined by different criteria to those that one would refer to in seeking to establish whether it is true that children are influenced by their peer groups.

I imagine that Hirst obviously does not mean anything like that, and that what he is thinking of are logically distinct ways of assessing different kinds of proposition regardless of the particular subject matter. I use the phrase 'different kinds of truth criteria' in order to avoid any ambiguity and to indicate, as Hirst himself suggests, that we are concerned with something like the distinction between an empirical proposition ('This picture weighs twelve pounds') and an aesthetic proposition ('This picture is beautiful'), the point being that in assessing the truth of each of these propositions different *kinds* of criteria would be needed, and not simply different criteria.

But if this interpretation of Hirst is correct, then surely there are only two forms of knowledge, the empirical being one and the aesthetic being merely a specific example of the other, which I have elsewhere generically termed philosophical.[13] My suggestion is thus similar to that of A. J. Watt, who argues that there are only two systems of what he calls rational belief.[14] First there is the purely conceptual system which is governed only by norms of logical consistency. Secondly there is the factual system which is governed both by the norms of logical consistency and by the observable facts of the matter. In other words, if you want to know whether a particular proposition is true or false there are fundamentally only two ways of proceeding, the appropriate way being decided by the nature of the proposition. With some propositions one can only employ reasoned logic; with others one may also employ empirical demonstration.

So far I have merely asserted a contrary position to that of Hirst. I hope that my position will become clearer, and also be seen to be more cogent than Hirst's, if we now examine Hirst's eight proposed forms of knowledge. Just how distinct are they, and in what ways?

In my view the physical and the human sciences both become examples of the empirical form of knowledge. So too does history conceived of as a straightforward attempt to establish what happened in the past. Many of course would not accept this simplified conception of history as truly history at all, and some sociologists might jib at the suggestion that their contribution to the human sciences can be confined to the search for empirical truth. But arguing about the proper conception of history or sociology is a separate matter and will not affect the present issue. If, for the present, we conceive of sociology as the attempt to establish true propositions about human behaviour and the nature of human society, and history as the attempt to establish true propositions about occurrences in the past, then both, like the physical sciences, are empirical pursuits or, in Watt's terminology, factual systems of belief. For each of these disciplines seeks to arrive at true propositions by means of consistent reasoning applied to empirical evidence.

It is true that these three disciplines are distinguishable and that they are so in a number of ways. Some, for instance, would seek to distinguish history from science on the grounds that scientific enquiry begins with an hypothesis which is then subjected to empirical test, whereas historical enquiry begins with observation of the evidence and then deduces an explanation. Furthermore, differences in the nature of the evidence relevant to each of these disciplines certainly leads to different problems in seeking for truth and to different degrees of probability. But these differences do not lead to the conclusion that each discipline involves different *kinds* of criteria for assessing truth. In each sphere the criteria are of the same kind : logical consistency and compatibility with the observable facts.

What then can Hirst mean by the claim that they are distinct forms of knowledge? Only that they are distinguishable theoretical activities, which are not further reducible in the same way as his so-called fields of knowledge, such as geography, are. As far as the distinction between at least some of his forms of knowledge and fields of knowledge goes, I am in agreement with Hirst. That is to say, geography, as it is usually understood, may legitimately be seen as a composite entity held together by its subject matter and involving such disciplines as science, sociology and history. History, sociology and the physical sciences are certainly irreducible in a way that geography is not. But the fact remains that by the same criteria as history, the physical sciences and the human sciences are distinguishable, we must make further distinctions between chemistry, biology, physics, psychology, sociology and so on. And indeed these things *are* distinct. The question is whether there are criteria which will at one and the same time serve to show that the human sciences can be distinguished from history and the physical sciences, without involving a similar distinction between sociology, psychology, chemistry and so on.

In order to establish that ideally all individuals ought to be initiated into his eight forms of knowledge, Hirst needs to establish, at least, that if an individual is unaware of, say, the nature of the social sciences there will be a number of propositions the truth or falsehood of which he will not be able to understand how to set about assessing. My claim is that, if he understands the nature of what I term the empirical form of knowledge, then he is in a position to understand the nature of the human sciences. He will not, of course, be a proficient human scientist as a result of being a competent physical scientist. But then he will not be a proficient chemist as a result of being a competent physicist.

Mathematics and philosophy, on the other hand, make no appeal to the empirical. They may of course in practice be applied to the empirical world and proceed with reference to empirical facts. Thus one may employ mathematics in engineering, or philosophise about how men ought to live, taking good account of how men appear to be constituted as a matter of psychological fact. But whether a mathematical proposition is true or false is entirely decided by its consistency, or lack of it, with a system of other interrelated propositions. Similarly philosophical discussion about whether the table on which I think that I am now leaning exists, depends upon suspending one's normal conviction that the fact that I can see it and feel it effectively puts an end to the discussion. The question, if you like, is precisely whether empirical evidence is reliable, from which it is clear that empirical evidence can play no part in determining the truth or falsehood of the philosophical question of whether this table truly exists.

In my view then mathematics and philosophy are both examples of the philosophic form of knowledge or Watt's conceptual system of belief. Once again they are of course distinguishable in a number of ways as theoretical disciplines, but they do not appear to involve different kinds of criteria for truth, except in the sense that, involving different subject matter, they naturally refer to different data. Any distinction between them along the lines that Hirst seems to suggest would involve a corresponding distinction between trigonometry, geometry, philosophy of art, logic and so on.

And what of literature and the fine arts, religion and morals? How these come to be forms of knowledge on Hirst's criteria is perhaps the most puzzling feature of his theory. What, in the first place, counts as a *bona fide* fine arts proposition, or even a *bona fide* religious or moral proposition? If Michelangelo's David in some sense expresses a proposition (which I think is what Hirst means rather than that one may make aesthetic judgements about it), then I for one am simply at a loss as to how the truth of such a 'proposition' may be assessed in any way that remotely parallels what he seemed to mean in the context of the physical sciences, mathematics and the other forms so far considered. If on the other hand he is thinking of aesthetic propositions (as when he claims to be concerned with developing 'the ability to recognise empirical assertions or aesthetic judgements for what they are') these would seem to be clearly a branch of philosophy. Granted that there is room for heated debate over whether philosophers, who may have no familiarity with art as such, are in a position to write books on aesthetics, as they sometimes do – granted that, the fact remains that whether it is true that Michelangelo's David is beautiful is at least partly a philosophical question. Whether it is true depends on what we mean by a 'true proposition' and what we mean by 'beautiful' as much as on an accurate perception of the features of the work.[15]

This raises a second major problem: Hirst's classification seems to beg the enormous question of whether religious, aesthetic and moral propositions can be true. Some would certainly argue that the most interesting feature of these areas is precisely that they admit of no criteria for determining truth or falsehood. Can a proposition such as 'God exists' be assessed as true or false by any criteria?

It is not clear, then, precisely what Hirst means by labelling these three areas as forms of knowledge. On my view, where they belong depends on what kind of propositions we are thinking of in each sphere. One can ask empirical or non-empirical questions in each sphere. For example, one can ask whether people believe in God or whether God exists, whether a certain moral value is subscribed to, or whether it ought to be, and whether a painting exhibits observance of the Golden Curve or whether the fact that it does makes it beautiful. The first of each pair of questions belongs to the empirical form of knowledge, the second to the philosophical. Whether the second of each pair can be answered at all must remain an open question, but it is certain that its truth, if it can be determined, will not be determined by empirical means.

In short I claim that all propositions fall exhaustively into one of two categories by reference to the kinds of criteria appropriate to establishing their truth or falsity: those that are partially dependent on empirical considerations for their resolution, and those that are not.

In summarising what I have said so far, it should be stressed that we are concerned here with a question of truth and not with a question of convenience. There is a distressing tendency for critics of Hirst to base their argument on an estimate of how useful his classification scheme will prove to be for curriculum construction. In some instances it may be legitimate to compare classification schemes of knowledge with respect to their usefulness. But it can only be so on two prior assumptions: first, that the two schemes being compared are valid and not just mistaken or incoherent, and secondly, *a fortiori*, that they are different *kinds* of classification. If two schemes of classification are supposed to be of the same kind but are in fact different, then one of them at least must be at fault in some way, and their comparative 'usefulness' is nothing to the point. What is wrong is not, in the final analysis, a great deal of use.

Thus it may perhaps be legitimate to compare the relative usefulness for curriculum planning of Phenix's realms of meaning and Hirst's forms of knowledge.[16] For it could be argued that both are valid and that each is concerned with a different kind of classification, the two being mutually compatible. But it is not legitimate to proceed, as Whitfield tends to do, as if the choice between Peterson's 'modes of thinking' and Hirst's 'forms of knowledge' were essentially a matter of administrative convenience.[17] Nor does Warwick get the emphasis right when he writes : 'the reaction of the individual teacher to integrated studies must stem from the view he takes of education as a whole. Is the purpose of the school an initiation into what Hirst would call "Forms of Knowledge" . . . ? If so, then the subject based curriculum will probably be favoured'.[18] The primary question is not whether one happens to think that the school should initiate children into what Hirst happens to call 'forms of knowledge', but whether the nature of knowledge is such as Hirst claims it to be – whether what Hirst says is comprehensible, coherent and *true*. (Incidentally, there is no necessary reason why those who believe that Hirst is correct should favour a subject-centred curriculum.)

The situation is simply this : Hirst claims that there are eight forms of knowledge, the most striking defining characteristic of each being that it gives rise to logically unique kinds of proposition which have their own kinds of truth criteria. Examples of propositions matching the forms (based on Whitfield)[19] might be :

1 The opposite angles of a parallelogram are equal.   (Mathematics)
2 A current of 1 amp is flowing in this circuit.   (Physical sciences)
3 Charles I's persistent belief in his divine rights led to his death. (History)
4 Children's values are formed more through their home background than through the school.   (Human sciences)
5 Michelangelo's David (or, alternatively, Michelangelo's David is a superb work of art).[20]   (Fine arts)
6 It is wrong to interfere with people's freedom.   (Morals)
7 The Pope is infallible.   (Religion)
8 'Good' is a simple notion, just as 'yellow' is a simple notion. (Philosophy)

The essence of Hirst's argument must be that the way in which one needs to proceed to establish the truth or falsehood of each of these propositions is logically quite distinct, such that if one was not familiar with any propositions of a certain type or corresponding to one of the eight listed, one would be completely unaware of a particular kind of procedure appropriate and necessary to examining the truth or falsehood of certain propositions. It is not sufficient to his purposes to point out that, for instance, one could not say whether the second proposition is true or false without some familiarity with physics. For on that basis one would have to add countless other types of proposition and hence forms of knowledge. One could not examine the question of whether it is true or false that 'No picture can be saved by toning, but a good enlargement may be ruined if toned unwisely' without some familiarity with photography.

What Hirst is maintaining, therefore, is that, though subject matter may vary, and hence we may sometimes be at a loss as to whether a particular statement is true or false, because we are unfamiliar with the subject matter, there are also these eight distinct kinds of procedure for testing the truth of different kinds of proposition. Familiarity with the eight forms provides a necessary condition for examining any currently conceivable proposition for truth or falsehood. Such familiarity is not of course a sufficient condition: we might be unfamiliar with the subject matter or simply fail to recognise what form a particular proposition should be classified under. But it is a necessary condition.

If Hirst is correct in saying that there are these eight distinct kinds of procedure, then it follows that familiarity with them is a necessary condition of being able to assess the truth or falsity of propositions. And he would have a very strong case for arguing that schools should initiate children into the forms. We cannot realistically hope to introduce them to all subject matter, but we could introduce them to this necessary condition of coping adequately with any kind of proposition. Any individual who lacked familiarity with one or more forms, would *ipso facto*, if Hirst is right, be incapable of assessing the truth or falsity of any propositions relating to those forms.

My contention is that Hirst is wrong. Ignoring the question of varying subject matter and concepts (by which criteria alone we should arrive at hundreds of forms), the propositions listed fall firmly into two groups by the criterion of validation procedures. The truth or falsehood of (2), (3) and (4) is to be arrived at by a combination of logic and reference to empirical evidence. The truth or falsehood of the other propositions, if their truth or falsehood can be established at all, can only be determined by logical reasoning. If an individual knows how to set about examining whether 'The Pope is infallible' is true or false, then he is familiar with the kind of analytic procedure that I call philosophical and which is necessary for examining the truth or falsity of (1), (6) and (8). Similarly if he knows how to set about assessing whether (4) is true or false, then he is familiar with the kind of procedure necessary to examining whether (2) and (3) are true or false. He will not necessarily be able to give an informed opinion as to whether (2) and (3) are true or false, since he may not have studied physics or history. But as far as that goes nobody can make informed comments about photography, pop music, cricket, astrology or anything else, if they have not studied the subject matter.

This said, there does seem to be something fundamental about most at least of Hirst's eight forms of knowledge. Could it be that some of them are fundamental for different kinds of reasons? Such, at any rate, might appear to be the implication of the use of the expression 'modes of knowledge and experience' rather than 'forms of knowledge' by Hirst in later accounts of his theory.[21] What I now want to suggest, without specific reference to Hirst, is that, besides the two forms of knowledge that I have outlined, there are also two basic *interpretative attitudes* to the world and a number of distinct *kinds of awareness*.

By a basic interpretative attitude to the world I mean a fundamental conception of what the world is about, or a view as to the terms in which existence is ultimately to be explained. At rock bottom there seem to me to be only two such interpretative attitudes, which I shall label the religious and the scientific. All I am drawing attention to here is the distinction between someone to whom the mystery of life is ultimately only explicable in some religious terms, and someone to whom this kind of explanation is unnecessary and meaningless. To this latter person there is no mystery, merely a degree of ignorance which is in principle capable of final resolution by scientific enquiry.

I am not suggesting that respect for science and a religious interpretative attitude are necessarily incompatible. Nor do I wish to confine the term 'religious' to any particular set of beliefs or any particular creed. I classify as a religious interpretative attitude any view of the world that depends upon fundamental axioms that are not scientifically demonstrable. Thus an Hegelian or a Marxist position involves a religious rather than a scientific interpretative attitude. The distinction, in crude terms, is between those who see life as a whole as something that is entirely in man's hands, to make what he will of, and those who, whether as a result of commitment to a God, a law of destiny or whatever, do not.

How many distinct kinds of awareness there are I am not certain. Nor am I very happy about the term. What I am trying to refer to are different kinds of feeling or sentiment that contemplation of some phenomena may arouse. Thus we can certainly distinguish between moral and aesthetic feeling. Some experiences, situations, scenes or occurrences provoke moral awareness, some aesthetic awareness, and obviously some may provoke both or neither, depending on the nature of the individual in question. Presumably we should add a religious kind of awareness and a scientific kind of awareness, this latter being marked by a concern for the facts of the matter rather than by moral, aesthetic or religious sentiment. Religious and scientific awareness are obviously not to be confused with a religious or scientific interpretative attitude; one may have a religious interpretative attitude, yet contemplate a particular situation scientifically.

The problem comes in knowing where to draw a line. Should one refer, for instance, to an historical kind of awareness? And if so, what about a biological or a psychological awareness? Tentatively, my answer would be that though of course a biologist may look with different eyes on a pond than one who is biologically ignorant, there is no peculiarly biological sentiment. His biological knowledge allows him to experience a scientific awareness, that others might not be able to experience, and he may, of course, as an individual rather than a biologist, experience religious or aesthetic awareness. Similarly I would deny that it makes much sense to refer to a psychological kind of awareness, akin to an aesthetic or moral kind of awareness. Where this leaves history I am uncertain.

Now I must stress that nothing hangs on these observations in themselves. We must recall the process by which we arrived at this juncture. Hirst argued that education should be concerned to develop the rational mind. His argument itself did not appear to be conclusive, but I do not think that it will prove very difficult to argue convincingly that ideally every individual ought to be capable of distinguishing whatever forms of knowledge there are. The trouble is that there only appear to be two forms of knowledge, if we define a form of knowledge by reference to a logically distinct way of assessing the truth of its propositions. The distinction between the empirical and philosophical form of knowledge will not give us very much help in constructing a curriculum.

I then added, what I take to be an indisputable truth, that one can distinguish what I called the religious and the scientific interpretative attitude, and that in addition there are at least four distinct kinds of awareness or distinguishable types of sentiment: the moral, aesthetic, religious and scientific. That claim also is supposed to be beyond dispute. It will be seen that most of Hirst's forms are included in my forms, my interpretative attitudes or my kinds of awareness. But it should not be assumed that at this stage I am saying that anything automatically follows for the curriculum. Even if Hirst's argument for initiating children into the forms of knowledge were satisfactory, it would not apply, on my view, to most of his forms, since they are not forms of knowledge at all. But in the final chapter I shall argue that there is good reason to initiate children into the two forms of knowledge, the two interpretative attitudes and the four kinds of awareness. That is why I have introduced the terms here.

IV   CHILD-CENTRED CURRICULA

So far all the approaches to the curriculum that I have considered have had in common the assumption that there are certain things which it is worthwhile for children to engage in because of something about those things themselves, rather than because of anything about the children. They may thus all be regarded as subject-centred curriculum theories.[22] Some very silly people will say that that is enough to condemn them. This is not so. Nor is it true that 'unless actual situations involving children can become child-centred they cannot be educational',[23] unless we arbitrarily make it true by definition. The only way to demonstrate the inadequacy of subject-centred theories is to examine them one by one and show in what way they are unsatisfactory, as I have attempted to do in the previous pages. But it must be stressed that I would not claim to have shown that the specific opinions about what children should study or do, put forward by Nisbet, Bantock, Peters and Hirst, are necessarily unacceptable. I have not been trying to establish that conclusion. It may yet turn out that we can argue for the intrinsic value or for the educational value of certain activities. It may be that some or all of the specific activities mentioned (science, philosophy, literature, typing, etc.) are worthwhile. All I would claim at this point is that none of the arguments considered could claim to have established beyond reasonable doubt that we ought to initiate children into these various activities.

I shall turn now to consideration of some child-centred theories. I use the term 'child-centred' curriculum theory loosely to refer to any theory that is not based on the assumption that there are certain activities, pursuits or subjects which just are intrinsically or extrinsically worthwhile, regardless of what any particular individual may feel about them. The most obvious examples of this kind of theory are those that involve the claim that a worthwhile curriculum can be constructed solely by reference to the needs, interests and/or wants of the individual child.

I do not intend to cover ground here that has been painstakingly covered elsewhere, and where there is really no room for disagreement or debate.[24] Thus I shall not discuss the ambiguity in the claim that the curriculum should be based on children's interests. It is at once obvious that the phrase 'based on' is imprecise and might mean 'solely by reference to' or 'with due regard for', and that the latter begs the question of how much attention to children's interests amounts to 'due regard'. It is also obvious that 'based on children's interests' might mean either based on what is in their interests or on what actually interests them. The claim that the curriculum should be based on what is in children's interests would presumably not be disputed by anybody. But it is only uncontentious, because, being purely formal, it is unhelpful. All would agree that the curriculum should be in the interests of children, but that merely leads on to the question of what is in the interests of children. In short the claim that the curriculum should be based on children's interests is only significant and worth considering, if we take it to mean that the content of the curriculum, what is actually done or studied, should be determined more or less exclusively by the actual interests of particular children.

Similarly I do not need to say much about 'needs'. All will agree that the curriculum should be constructed by reference to children's needs, if that is taken to mean that a curriculum should not ignore children's needs. But once again we have only a formal and not very helpful rule of thumb. What do children actually need? How are we to determine that? No one can dispute, I think, that the logic of the term 'need' is such that reference to a need presupposes an objective. I only need food on the assumption that I want to stay alive, for example. This being so, any attempt to draw up a list of children's needs will either produce some important but highly contentious claims, or else a list of basic needs that are also rather boring and trivial. For example, most of us will agree that children need love, security, shelter, food and such like. But we only agree because we share some broad objective to the effect that the individual should be alive, healthy and adjusted. And a list of needs of this sort is not going to help us plan a curriculum to any marked extent. On the other hand, if I were to suggest that children need to be initiated into the forms of knowledge, we should have a significant but highly contentious curriculum sugges- tion. In order to establish that children really *need* such initiation, I would have to show that its results were desirable in some way. Such a task, besides being complex, would take me way beyond talk of 'needs'. I therefore conclude that the suggestion that the curriculum should be based on children's needs is not in itself of any practical help.

This brings us to wants, and the first question to be asked is whether there is a distinction to be drawn between an individual's wants and interests. If I want to do something, must I necessarily be interested in doing it? If I am interested in doing it, must I necessarily want to do it? Provided that we are concentrating for the moment only on the idea of wanting to do something or being interested in something for its own sake, I should have thought that the answer to both questions is 'yes'. It is surely inconceivable that I should want to play football, go for a walk or read a book, if I were not interested in doing these things. (If we forget the proviso, the matter is different: I might very well want to read a book for some further end, such as the acquisition of informa- tion, without being interested in reading the book.) And it is equally odd to suggest that a person might be interested in doing these things without also wanting to do them. This being the case a curriculum based on children's actual and immediate wants would be equivalent to a curriculum based on their actual interests.

What is to be said about this approach to the curriculum? The first point to clear up is the distinction between proposing that children's interests should provide the starting point for a curriculum, and the proposal that they should govern the whole content of the curriculum. The former suggestion effectively reduces interests to a motivational role. On this view the school has predetermined objectives and some predetermined content that it wishes to impart to children, but it approaches the content by means of the children's actual present interests. The argument for such an approach would presumably be based on the empirical claim that this method is more effective than the alternative procedure of trying directly to interest children in a previously determined curriculum. Since, therefore, it is in essence a methodological claim, and says nothing about how one might determine the objectives and content that the child is ultimately supposed to attain by way of his interests, we need not pursue it here.

The theory that really needs examining is the view that a worthwhile curriculum would be one that consisted almost exclusively of taking up and exploring children's actual interests. Would such a curriculum be worthwhile? It might be argued that this is the approach to the curriculum we should adopt, on the grounds that nobody has produced an argument to show that any activities are intrinsically worthwhile. That being so, we have no right to proceed as if some activities just are worthwhile, and should rather respect individual preferences. But this argument clearly will not do. In the first place, even if we accept that we have not yet found, and are not likely to find, an argument that establishes the intrinsic value of certain activities, it does not follow automatically that this theory is acceptable. At present we have no *more* reason to accept it as true that a curriculum based on children's interests is worthwhile, than we have to accept that a curriculum based on Hirst's forms of knowledge is worthwhile. Secondly, even if we were to accept a thesis to the effect that the value of an activity lies in the individual's interest in it, it is surely clear that we would need to draw a distinction between children and adults. This brings me on to a second argument.

It may be said that such a curriculum must be worthwhile because the sole criterion for estimating the worth of an activity is one's interest in it. There are variations of the argument, which I shall examine later, that have considerable plausibility. But as it stands, it is surely preposterous. Common sense revolts at the idea that the fact that a person is interested in doing something makes that activity, whatever it is, worthwhile. It is simply not plausible to suggest that if I were genuinely interested in torturing small boys that alone would make it worthwhile. Furthermore, such slight plausibility as the thesis may have is surely dependent to some extent on the notion that people's interests are based on some knowledge, foresight and experience. That is to say it is slightly more plausible to suggest that what an average adult, who has some idea of alternatives open to him, some inkling of the consequences of various activities, some range of abilities, and some experience of various activities, wants to do, is for that reason worthwhile, than it is to suggest that the average young child's wants are necessarily worthwhile.

Let us not mess about on this issue. If anybody were to make the straightforward claim, as some educationalists appear to be, that what the individual child wants is by the mere fact of his wanting it worthwhile, it would follow that that person would have to accept this consequence: if, for whatever reason, a nine-year-old child wanted to commit murder, that action would be worthwhile. Conversely, anybody who finds that conclusion ludicrous must reject the premiss.

Why have I used such an extreme, emotive and implausible example? Deliberately, in order to force the issue. Presumably the advocate of education according to children's wants, if he is going to explain himself at all, will now bring in some kind of qualification. Perhaps he will say that wants that interfere with other people's wants are illegitimate; or that no child would want to do this, if he understood the nature and consequences of the act; or that no child would want to do this, had he not been brought up in seriously inadequate and deprived surroundings; or that this is immoral behaviour and that 'wants' should be subordinated to considerations of moral behaviour; or, pathetically, that my example is a typical philosophic *reductio ad absurdum*, indicating the general irrelevance of philosophy to the practical business of living (and dying).

But, whatever is said, the tough fact remains that the simplistic thesis that the curriculum should be geared to the child's wants is radically altered. It turns out that the theory as given was not quite complete: we were given the harmless and trivial part, and told nothing about the vital and complex part. Everybody would agree that the child should do what he wants, *with qualifications*. The question is what are the qualifications to be?

What if we say that immoral behaviour must be discouraged, even when children want to engage in it? Do we not have an enormous problem on our hands of determining what counts as immoral behaviour? And is it anyway as easy as that? Is there not some behaviour that we might regard as immoral, but sometimes think it best to allow children to indulge in, at least for a period of time? And what are we

to make of the claim that wants should be thwarted only when they involve interference with the wants of others? Does one child's wanting
silence in which to read interfere with a second's wanting to make a
noise, or should we say that it is the second child's want that interferes
with the wants of the first child?

I am leaving out of account any consideration of the suggestion that,
quite apart from the sort of extreme example I have taken, we owe it
to children to *expand* their potential range of wants, and to equip them
with the wherewithal to indulge a variety of 'wants' which they might
not otherwise be able to experience. I ignore that important line of
argument, because it should by now be clear that the claim that children
should do what they want, because their wanting to do something makes
it worthwhile, is absurd.

The final variant of the 'wants' thesis is, I suspect, the version that
most of its proponents would finally retreat to. This is the claim not that
what interests the child is *ipso facto* worthwhile, but that, as a matter
of fact, left to their own devices, children want to do or are interested
in doing worthwhile things. Thus, reverting to the example, the desire
to kill is the result of various repressive features of the child's environment, and would not have occurred in happier circumstances.

This thesis forms one strand of Rousseau's *Emile*.[25] It is not the only
strand in that puzzling book, for Rousseau's use of the term 'nature',
which carries the burden of his argument, is nothing if not equivocal.
Sometimes he appears to mean' by 'the natural behaviour' that he is
anxious to see in Emile, behaviour that is spontaneous. Sometimes he
appears to mean behaviour that conforms to his notion of how men
used to behave in pre-civilised times. (Of course those two senses of
natural behaviour become synonymous, if we presume a pre-civilised
age. But in anything roughly approximating to civilised society, by
which I here mean little more than organised social life as opposed to
instinctive individualism, there may obviously be a distinction between
the spontaneous behaviour of the social animal, and the sort of behaviour he would have indulged in if he were not a social animal.) And
sometimes, as when he refers to Sophie's natural role, he appears to
have in mind nothing more than a customary and conventional social
role.[26] Rousseau also plays upon the normative use of the term 'natural',
as when we refer to something as natural as opposed to unnatural,
meaning more or less that it is good or desirable.

The upshot of all this is that it is difficult at any given point to be
sure whether Rousseau's claim is that a certain feature of his education is good because it involves spontaneity, good because it conforms
to pre-civilised practice, good because it conforms to socially accepted
norms, or good because it is, in his view, good. But certainly a sig-

nificant part of his general educational perspective would appear to be the claim that, left alone, without adult interference or imposition beyond the point of ensuring a natural environment, the child will develop in such a way as rapidly to acquire knowledge and social virtues when he is 'ready' to in his late teens.

A similar thesis is common in some Utopian literature, notably in Aldous Huxley's *Island* and William Morris's *News from Nowhere*. But the most famous practitioner of something approaching this theory was A. S. Neill.[27] This is not the place to engage in a detailed critique of Neill's published theorising. The basic features of his theory are plainly exhibited in the practice of his school Summerhill. And it is clear that Neill's view involves the claim that at least generally, even allowing for unpropitious home backgrounds and so on, children left for the most part to their own devices, will come in time to live worthwhile lives.

That last sentence must, I think, stand as one of the fairest summaries of Neill's position ever written. I have not criticised, as well one might, his doctrine that the child is born good; I have not treated his theory as though its merit depended upon one hundred per cent effectiveness; and I have not tried to commit him to the thesis that all that Summerhill children do is good and worthwhile, which he certainly would not have maintained. But he obviously did maintain – indeed how could he sensibly not do so in the circumstances – that the consequences of letting children do more or less what they wanted was that they grew up to lead worthwhile lives.

The problem in this thesis should be at once apparent. It involves two elements: first a view of what constitutes a worthwhile life, and secondly the empirical claim that as a matter of fact Summerhill pupils live worthwhile lives as adults. There is, however, no hard empirical evidence to establish or refute this claim. This is hardly surprising since in the nature of things it is difficult to conduct surveys into the question of whether people are living worthwhile lives, or even whether they think they are. But the crucial point lies in the fact that no such enquiry could even in principle be launched, without prior understanding of what constitutes a worthwhile life. If the claim is the empirical one that education geared to children's wants leads to a situation in which they live worthwhile lives, which presumably means engage in worthwhile activities, then we have not avoided or answered the question of what makes something worthwhile. It may, in short, be true that by and large education does not need to initiate children into worthwhile activities, since they will enter into them when they want to, but we could only know that if we knew what activities were worthwhile. Conversely if we were to see reason to regard certain things as worthwhile, say, for the sake of example, philosophy, science and typing, then it is far from clear that it is empirically true that most individuals would come to these things of their own accord in their own time. If we say that such activities are only worthwhile if the individual wants to engage in them, then we revert to the previous variant of the 'wants' theory which has already proved to be unsatisfactory.

The wants and interests of children may obviously be of some importance to the educator. Grounds could be produced for saying that it would be both wrong and unwise to ride roughshod over them as a matter of policy. And no doubt, very often, by concentrating on children's actual wants or interests it is possible for the teacher to help them find aspects of value in those wants or interests. But there does not seem to be any case for saying that an activity is necessarily worthwhile if the child wants to engage in it, and the suggestion that children will as a matter of fact come to select the worthwhile of their own accord presupposes an answer to the question at issue: 'What is worthwhile and what makes it so?' From which we must conclude that it has not been shown that a worthwhile curriculum can be constructed by reference to children's wants or interests alone.

V DESCHOOLING[28]

Despite the conclusion of the previous section, I turn now to a very similar thesis – perhaps it is actually the same thesis in a different language – as representative of the *nouvelle vogue* in educational theory. Paul Goodman, sometimes referred to as 'one of the most outspoken radicals in contemporary American education',[29] must stand here as representative of those curriculum theories which are based on the premiss that the curriculum must be dismantled and compulsory schooling replaced by multiple options (none of which need necessarily be taken up by the individual). Consideration of Goodman will allow me to bring to the fore a dimension or aspect of education that is often largely ignored – namely, its political or social consequences. For the most obvious problem in Goodman's argument is not, as with most of the theories so far considered, some logical weakness, but the social consequences of accepting his proposals.

'We can, I believe,' Goodman writes, 'educate the young entirely in terms of their free choice.'[30] He therefore proposes that there should be no prearranged curriculum up to the age of twelve. This means, for example, that there is to be no presumption that it would be particularly desirable for a child to be able to read by the age of twelve, and presumably, therefore, many would not in fact be able to do so. But Goodman believes that the value of functional literacy is generally exaggerated anyway. It is, he suggests, 'the attitude . . . that counts',[31] and the creative will go their own way of their own accord. I take it that he means by this that those who have some inner compulsion to write poetry, or whatever, will feel that compulsion, will pick up the skills of reading and writing of their own volition, and would only have been 'hampered' by school lessons related to poetry anyway. Similarly, I presume that the 'attitude' which counts for more than 'reading ability' is an attitude of interest in literature. What matters is whether you care about the written word : if you do, you will take steps to master it; if you do not, there is no particular value in such mastery.

'In the adolescent and college years . . . the correct policy would be to open as many diverse paths as possible.'[32] Goodman reckons on about fifteen per cent of children, those who 'can learn well by books and study in an academic setting',[32] choosing to go to secondary school. For the rest he advocates self-help and immersion in some apprenticeship. Academic credits he dismisses as irrelevant and discouraging in relation to such things as social work, architecture and pedagogy. Modern languages can be learnt abroad. Taking an idea from the Ancient Greeks, he recommends that the *polis* (city) itself should be the educational environment.

He concedes that 'voluntary adolescent choices are often random and foolish, and usually transitory; but', he claims, without indicating quite why he does so, 'they are the likeliest ways of growing up reasonably'.[33] To demonstrate his basic contention that schooling is not essential, Goodman observes that 'we were not exactly savages in 1900 when only 6% of adolescents graduated from High School'.[34]

Goodman's argument is slightly obscured by his tendency to throw in contentious value judgements ('Increasingly, the best young people resolutely resist authority') and emotive language ('Young men learn more about the theory and practice of government by resisting the draft than they ever learned in Political Science 412.' Is that true? How do you know?). Nonetheless, there *is* an argument. The first question is how convincing is it? In relation to that question I offer a few observations.

Of course modern languages can be learnt abroad, if you can afford to go abroad or have the talents to gain employment abroad. And of course much can be learnt as a result of the individual taking it upon himself to learn, if he knows what there is to be learnt, if he has some aptitude for schooling himself, and if he can read! But is there not a danger that Goodman's approach to education would fail to provide in some cases for these necessary conditions? And is there not something rather curious about this approach which does not even trouble itself to ask whether modern languages are worth learning anyway? It simply observes that people *can* learn things without the aid of schools. It does not show that they will and it does not really face the question of whether that matters in respect of specific activities.

An important premiss in the thesis as a whole therefore has to be the claim that 'nothing can be . . . learned at all . . . unless it meets need, desire, curiosity or fantasy'.[35] If that were true, it would at least follow that there was no point in compulsory schooling, except where children felt such need, etc. If they *did* feel such need, then the schooling would not have to be compulsory. But there do not appear to be any obvious grounds for accepting that the premiss is true. Possibly we learn 'best', in some sense, what we desire to learn. But what does 'best' mean in this context? Where is the evidence for such an assertion? It surely flies in the face of a matter of simple experience: most of us have learned and remembered and understood things which we did not consciously need or desire to learn, and which did not tickle our curiosity or fantasy, at the time of learning. Moreover Goodman's claim ignores a point referred to in the previous section: it is possible for one person to provoke interest, desire, curiosity, etc. in another, and it might thus be argued that this is what schools should seek to do.

The suggestion that the *polis* should be educational is, I should have thought, either contradictory to the general thesis, or else wildly unrealistic. It is unrealistic if any direct comparison with Greek city states is intended. Chicago, for all its merits, just isn't Periclean Athens. It is true, or at any rate Thucydides makes Pericles say that it is true,[36] that Athens was itself an educational agency. The community way of life itself contributed something to the education of the individual. But that was dependent on a number of factors that no longer apply, such as the small size of the community and the fact that this 'education' was the privilege of a leisured minority who depended for subsistence on slave labour. Above all, education through the *polis* followed and was dependent on schooling: community education came through such things as attendance at the theatre to see and discuss plays that were written on themes that had been drummed into each member of the audience at school or at his mother's knee; it came through meeting and talking in the *agora* so that you could not avoid contact with a Socrates or a Sophocles. Finally, there was less need for organised schooling in such a city-state because there wasn't very much to know.[37]

If these points are granted and the idea of education through the *polis* is modified to suit changed conditions, then surely we have to envisage a more determined effort to set up 'agencies', whereby education might be disseminated. Such an agency is precisely what the school is supposed to be. If we now recall the basic suggestion, that individual children should be free to attend such 'agencies' when and if they feel like it, it is clear that education will not necessarily take place through the *polis*. To ensure that it did, we should have to ensure that people attended educational agencies.

One final point worth making relates to Goodman's dismissive attitude to academic credits. Academic credits, as such, are certainly irrelevant to social work or anything else. And if the argument is that possession of a certificate with distinction in education does not make a good teacher, I imagine we should all agree. But Goodman seems to mean more than this. He implies that the academic work which happens to result in a credit, certificate or what have you is also necessarily irrelevant to such things as being an architect, a social worker or a teacher. Specifically he claims that a teacher need only be trained in 'group therapy and, perhaps, a course in child-development'.[38]

This is not the place to discuss the merits or demerits of actual courses in teacher-training, social work and so on. That would be an entirely different question. But the general claim that there is no academic study that could benefit an architect or a social worker, or that a teacher need only know something about group therapy, seems frankly absurd. What would the teacher teach (for even in Goodman's scheme of things teachers, when called upon by interested students, are supposed to teach something)? How would a social worker begin to interpret a specific situation if he had no theoretical framework? How would the architect set about ensuring that his buildings did not fall down?

There are certainly problems then in Goodman's thesis, though they seem to arise more from the manner in which he presents it than from any fundamental logical flaw in the naked proposal that resources should be available for those who wish to make use of them. The real objection is surely that the adoption of such a proposal would lead to two nations within a community: the one consisting of the few – the medieval community of scholars – the other consisting of the majority – at best trained technocrats, at worst not even that. Each would in all probability disdain the way of life of the other, and the latter would be incapacitated for sharing the way of life of the former by the education, or lack of it, envisaged.

Goodman starts from what I imagine we may concede to be a true observation, that the present educational system involves enormous wastage, considerable failure, much worthless content and much sterility. But, as with many others who write educational books as a subversive activity, a reasonable perception of faults in the present system is not matched by a corresponding ability to offer anything better for the future. If there is wastage and worthless content today, then surely we must seek ways of avoiding wastage and find a worthwhile content for tomorrow. To dispense with compulsory schooling does not solve the problems of today: it shirks them. It says 'There will be no wastage, because there will be nobody there who might fail. There will be no worthless content, because there will be no content. There will be no bad schools, because there won't be any schools.'

It is all very well to observe that 'we were not exactly savages in 1900', but what we have to ask ourselves is whether we would welcome a return to the social conditions of 1900. For the vast majority of people at that time, to an even more significant degree than today, their way of life and the opportunities open to them were savagely circumscribed precisely because they lacked schooling. It does not, perhaps, have to be so, but the crucial and practical question is whether it would not be likely to be so. The trouble is that there simply is not one shred of evidence to support the assumption that by Goodman's means we provide 'the likeliest ways of growing up reasonably'. There is no reason to believe that such an approach to education 'tends' in the direction of the ideal *polis* which 'consists of worthwhile, attractive, and fulfilling callings and things to do'.[39]

Whereas, by contrast, it is a simple logical truth that people are in no position to choose to do what they do not understand, because they lack the skills or abilities which are necessary means to the ends in question. And there is plenty of hard evidence, to be culled from the experience of most of us, for the claim that there are activities which might have proved more rewarding to us than any we actually engage in, but which we are in no position even to try out, because we lack the necessary abilities.

In this section I have contented myself with pointing out that deschooling is likely in practice to lead to the emergence of two quite distinct classes and to a situation in which many unwittingly cut off their own options. I have implied, rather than systematically argued, that such consequences are undesirable. The argument for that judgement is contained, implicitly, in Part 2. By way of conclusion here, it may be left to the reader to marvel how such a backward-looking (on its own admission) and such a potentially divisive theory as Goodman's ever came to be called 'radical'.

VI THE HIDDEN CULTURE CURRICULUM THEORY

By 'the hidden culture curriculum theory' I mean the view that the curriculum should derive its content from the actual interests, pursuits and cultural values of the *social background* of the child in question. Such a theory has two points in common with the deschooling theory: it is regarded as radical by its proponents, and yet it seems inevitably to imply a social situation marked by an extreme division between two classes.

It is rather curious that this thesis should have emerged in recent years at all. For it seems to presuppose that all children in a school share the same cultural background at precisely the time that, thanks to comprehensivisation, this is supposed to be false. When reference is made to the actual cultural background of children, which it is suggested school curricula generally ignore, which children are we talking about? It may well be true that school curricula tend to embody a particular cultural stance, but it sometimes seems to be forgotten that for better or worse that cultural stance is the one also embodied in the backgrounds of a great many children. If the argument were simply that the individual's cultural background should be taken seriously and provide the basis of the curriculum, the conclusion would seem to be inescapable that we would need to reject a common system of schooling.

Some, of course, would accept this. Such a view bears a striking resemblance to T. S. Eliot's championship of the existence of a variety of thriving cultures in a community, which by the friction between them promote vigour and prevent inertia.[41] As against this it might be argued, as it was against Goodman, that such an educational policy would be catastrophically socially divisive, that it would deny individuals the opportunity of making a real choice between cultures (or aspects of cultures), and/or that some features at least of some cultures are not worth studying. But these arguments need not be pursued here, I think, for it seems clear that as a matter of fact those who put forward some variant of the hidden curriculum theory would be most offended at any suggestion that they can be compared to T. S. Eliot. On the contrary they see themselves as radical and anti-elitist. One concludes that they do not intend to suggest that children from different cultural backgrounds should be educated differently, which carries the corollary that even those children whose background enshrines the cultural values of the present school curriculum should not be allowed to perpetuate those values through education: a strong claim.

However, leaving aside confusion surrounding the question of for whom the curriculum is intended, we are presented with one reasonably clear thesis: the school curriculum is essentially dominated by certain cultural values, while it ignores or implicitly despises cultural values enshrined in the social background of the children. Somebody, never mind who, ought to be presented with a curriculum that enshrines the cultural values of that social background. I think that it is fair to say that the dominant values in the present curriculum may be equated with middle-class values and that the proposed values may be equated with working-class values. But it is difficult to be sure when one reads through the proposals of such proponents of the hidden culture theory as Jackson, Searle and Murdoch. I shall therefore try to avoid the terms 'middle' and 'working' class values.

A good example of this view, though perhaps not a very good example of a sustained argument for it, is provided by Graham Murdoch.[42] Murdoch claims that we are the victims of a conception of culture that has been imposed upon us. Basically that conception involves seeing culture as a collection of objects and masterpieces which most of us cannot hope to produce but only to admire. The objects and masterpieces are the traditionally accredited great paintings, great novels, etc. Who the 'we' are is never made clear. On the grounds that 'acceptance of available definitions necessarily entails a tacit support for the social order which they describe',[43] Murdoch redefines culture as 'the pattern of ideas, beliefs and values, through which people make sense of their experiences . . . and the various means through which they communicate this sense of themselves and their situation'.[43] He then devotes several paragraphs to trying to establish that 'the struggle by ordinary people to control the circumstances of their everyday lives' involved 'the attempt to resist dominant definitions'.[44]

All this is really rather tortuous and most peculiar. In no sense is it true that 'acceptance of available definitions necessarily entails a tacit support for the social order which they describe', although it well may generally happen to be the case that tacit support goes with acceptance of a definition. I can quite easily accept a definition of culture involving reference to certain accredited masterpieces, without valuing either that culture or whatever social order seeks to promote culture in that sense. I can just say that I am against culture. And to say that would be considerably less confusing than to redefine culture, as Murdoch does, in such a way that the same term is used to signify something quite different. For call it what you will, the notion of a body of accredited masterpieces is quite distinct from the notion of a way of life and its methods of communication. His conclusion seems to mean no more than that, historically, the working classes had their own distinctive sources of entertainment and resisted, finally with success, the attempts of middle-class do-gooders to dominate working men's clubs and to use them as platforms for 'propagating the assumptions and values of the dominant culture'.[45]

What has this to do with education? Murdoch's answer is that schools are now being used by the supporters of the dominant culture much as working men's clubs were originally used. 'Pupils have been given to understand that the finest and most valid forms of knowledge and expression are those developed by social and intellectual elites. Conversely, the cultural forms produced or enjoyed by subordinate groups have been classified as inferior and treated as non-negotiable currencies within the school system. Traditionally, therefore, the curriculum has enshrined the assumptions and forms of the dominant culture as the yardsticks against which other, contending cultures have been measured and found wanting.'[46] He illustrates this general claim by reference to two quotations, both of which are rather scathing about pop music.

That 'what goes on in schools is primarily determined . . . by the demands of dominant groups' seems to me to be an undeniable truth, since it is a tautology: if a group does not impose its will, it is not dominant. Furthermore it cannot be denied that the education of individual children is to some extent affected by such distant factors as the arbitrary whims of publishers, the views of examination boards, and institutionalised values such as 'competitiveness, regulating activity by the clock, working hard and productively'[47] (though what Murdoch means by claiming that these values belong only to the dominant social order and what his evidence is for this assertion, I am not sure).

But what is really wrong with this is the lack of specific reference to what is involved in the alternative suppressed culture, a corresponding lack of any argument to suggest why we should value it, and a similar lack of argument to show that the dominant culture is not worthwhile. In essence the argument appears to be as crude as this: 'What goes on in schools can be shown to stem from certain people's likes and dislikes – people who, incidentally, are powerful in society – therefore these things should not go on in schools.' Maybe they should not, but that line of reasoning is hardly persuasive.

The exception to my stricture that there is lack of specific reference is the reference to pop music. But clearly the mere assertion that 'pop music can . . . be a means through which people can deepen their awareness of themselves and their capacities, and extend their understanding and insight into the experiences of others'[48] is not an argument that establishes that pop music ought to be in the curriculum instead of, or even as well as, literature. It is not an argument at all. It is, I repeat, a mere assertion with which some might agree and others, even those of us who like and know pop music very well indeed, would not. Now if somebody could show by argument and research that the study of pop music (or merely the stimulation of pop music) could either meet the same objectives as the study of 'accredited masterpieces' of literature, or alternatively meet different objectives which could be shown by reasoning to be desirable, that would be a different matter entirely.

But that, though it may be true, has not been shown by Murdoch. Nor does it follow that certain pursuits should not remain in the curriculum solely because they were introduced by dominant groups. *How* things happen is in the last resort remarkably uninteresting. The important question is whether it is desirable that things are happening.

The fact, even if it is a fact, that the curriculum as we have it was 'imposed' can hardly be held against it by any author, be it Murdoch or myself, who would ideally like to impose an alternative. What matters is whether what is imposed is worthwhile or is imposed for good reasons.

Certainly we must accept that pop music, ways of communicating, and many other values and activities which loom large in the everyday life of many people have to a large extent been ignored by the curriculum. But to treat this as cause for complaint demands some argument designed to show that there is more value in devoting school time to those activities than there is in devoting time to other activities, including those traditionally associated with the curriculum. I do not say that this could not in the nature of things be done, although I know of no convincing example of its being done. But in order to do it, it would be necessary to resort to some specific account of what makes an activity educationally worthwhile. One would need, for example, not only to argue that 'pop music can . . . be a means through which people can deepen their awareness of themselves', but also that to develop self-awareness in this way was desirable. Ultimately, therefore, the proponent of the hidden culture theory of curriculum has to revert to something like one of the other categories considered in this chapter.[49]

VII J. P. WHITE'S CATEGORY DISTINCTIONS

John White argues, in *Towards a Compulsory Curriculum*, that 'what is intrinsically worthwhile is identifiable with what a person would on reflection want for its own sake'.[50] He is not persuaded of the validity of any argument designed to prove that some activities just are intrinsically valuable or worthwhile, and specifically rejects both the transcendental argument employed by Peters, and Hirst's attempt at justifying his proposed liberal education. He concludes that the task of education is to enable individuals to make a meaningful choice between various activities and ways of life. Thus he would distinguish between someone who devotes his life to what others might regard as trivial pursuits as a result of lack of understanding of any alternatives, and someone who devotes his life to the same activities in full knowledge of what he is doing. One may say, therefore, referring to White's identification of the worthwhile with what a person would on reflection want for its own sake, that he sees education as a means of rendering the 'reflection' in question meaningful. Education should provide the individual with understanding of alternative activities and ways of life. Although his thesis as a whole is based firmly on the belief that individuals should freely choose for themselves how they want to live (or what is worthwhile), he concludes, quite consistently, I think, that 'we are right to make [the child] unfree now so as to give him as much autonomy as possible later on'.[51]

There are many points of interest here. Some, such as the basic point that a choice made in ignorance of alternatives can scarcely count as genuine free choice, I shall take up and use myself in subsequent pages. Some, such as the analysis of the worthwhile and the question of what precisely White is doing here and what conclusions follow from the analysis, I shall examine in the next chapter.

The issue that concerns me here is the distinction between two kinds of activity that White now introduces. The argument so far, if accepted, would establish that ideally every individual ought to have understanding of all conceivable activities and ways of life : he would then be in a position to make a genuine autonomous choice about how to live his life. But obviously the ideal is unrealistic. Is there any way of distinguishing between activities or pursuits, in respect of their inclusion in the school curriculum, that does not involve saying that some are better, superior or more important than others? White cannot consistently claim that, say, maths ought to be taught rather than photography on the grounds that the former is in some way more valuable in itself as a pursuit, since his whole thesis is based on the belief that such an assertion is illegitimate. It is not for schoolmasters to insist on the validity of their belief that maths is more worthwhile than photography. It is for each individual to decide what he would on reflection want for its own sake. Are there, then, any criteria whereby we can sensibly distinguish between what should be in the curriculum and what should not, without smuggling in any reference to the alleged superior worth of certain activities or pursuits?

White thinks that there are. For, according to him, those activities that cannot be understood without some sort of learning 'can be divided, exhaustively, into two classes'.[52] In the first class, which he calls Category 1 activities, are included all those activities of which 'no understanding of what it is to want' the activity in question 'is logically possible without engaging in' the activity in question. Category 2 activities comprise all those activities of which 'some understanding of what it is to want' the activity in question 'is logically possible without engaging in' it.[53] In working out and explaining this distinction, he himself lists communication in general, engaging in pure mathematics, engaging in the physical sciences, appreciating works of art and philosophising, as Category 1 activities. As examples of Category 2 activities he lists speaking a foreign language, cricket (or other organised games), cookery, painting pictures, and being an accountant. For the record, it should be mentioned that White is not advocating the exclusion of all Category 2 activities from school life. His curriculum proposals include the suggestion that time should be divided between a compulsory common curriculum and a range of available options; many Category 2 activities may justifiably find their way into the curriculum as options. But the compulsory common curriculum, it is argued, should consist of Category 1 activities on the grounds that no one could possibly know what it was to want to engage in them, if they were not initially brought to engage in them under the guidance of somebody who knew what he was doing.

It seems then that White is claiming that an individual who had never played cricket, for example, could nonetheless have some understanding of what it is to want to play cricket, whereas it would be logically impossible for someone to understand what it is to want to philosophise if they had never done any philosophising. There are, I think, two severe problems in this thesis. The first concerns the Category 2 activities and the claim that understanding of what it is to want them is possible without engaging in them.

White introduces the distinction he wishes to make with reference to understanding what it is to *want* to philosophise, play cricket, etc. He rapidly moves away from this and begins to refer to understanding what it is to philosophise, play cricket, etc. This transition may, I think, be important and illegitimate. For, if his subsequent argument establishes anything, it is that one cannot understand what some activities involve without engaging in them. Now it is true that understanding what something is, or what it involves, is a necessary condition of understanding what it is to want to engage in it. In plain words, my judgement that I do not want to engage in nuclear physics research – assuming that to mean that I would not enjoy it – is meaningless if I do not know what nuclear physics is. It is comparable to the child who says that he does not want cabbage, when he has never tasted it. (In one sense it may still be true that the child does not want cabbage. It may be a fact that he is against the idea of eating it. But the point is that his judgement is based on ignorance.) But understanding what is involved in something is not a sufficient condition of understanding what it is to want to engage in it. I may have some understanding of what weight-lifting is, but not understand what others get out of it or what it is to want to engage in this activity.

White does deal with a very similar, if not identical, objection: namely the suggestion that none of the activities can be understood without learning to perform them. 'A cricket devotee may argue that one cannot really understand what it is to play cricket, until one has had plenty of experience at playing it : until then one can only grasp the externals, not the essence.'[54] White suggests, as against this, that one might very well grasp the essence of cricket through, for example, a vivid literary account of the game. But, he continues, this sort of argument 'is really beside the point. For what should be at issue is not whether one can gain a full understanding of cricket without playing it, but whether one can have some understanding of it . . . That one can is surely indisputable'.[55]

It is indeed indisputable that one can have some understanding of cricket, in the sense that one could talk about it and recognise it, without playing it. (Being able to give a formal account and recognising examples are the criteria of 'understanding' laid down, reasonably enough, by White.) But is that the point, as White insists? What he is surely missing or glossing over is that what the cricket devotee means by a 'real understanding' is not just a fuller understanding by White's criteria, but a different kind of understanding: an understanding of what people get out of it, what it is to want to engage in it. And this is crucial, for if it is conceded, as I should have thought it must be, that you never actually 'know what you're missing till you try', then, even if White can substantiate that some activities cannot be understood in any way at all except by engaging in them, he does not really have an argument. For although as a result of initiation into Category 1 activities and receiving explanation about Category 2 activities he would understand what all activities involved, he would still not be in a position to make a realistic assessment of whether he would enjoy actually engaging in any Category 2 activities. That that is the plain truth is, I should have thought, established for most of us by personal experience. I have known what it is both to play and watch football for over twenty years now. But it was not until I was forcibly dragged to watch Leicester City play (and lose to) Liverpool, at the end of the 1973/4 season, that I began to understand what it is to want to watch football. Now I am a fanatic supporter.

If an individual is not in a position to make a realistic assessment of whether he would enjoy engaging in Category 2 activities, then surely he is not in any real sense able to judge what he would on reflection want for its own sake? If it is agreed that what a man wants when drunk or unaware of alternatives does not count as 'what he would on reflection want', why should consideration be paid to what a man wants when he has never had the opportunity to see if he enjoys engaging in alternatives?

To conclude, first, it is true that there are some activities of which one can have some understanding without engaging in them, but it does not follow that one understands what it is to want to engage in them. Confusion probably lurks in the ambiguity of the phrase 'understanding what it is to want X'. If that is taken to mean 'having some idea of the pleasure to be derived from X', it certainly does not necessarily follow from an understanding of what is involved in X. On the other hand, if it means 'understanding what it is that is wanted by those who want X', then it not only follows but is actually entailed in understanding X. But if the latter interpretation is taken then it does not follow from the fact that one understands what it is to want X that one is in a position to make an informed choice about whether one would enjoy doing X.

The second question focuses on Category 1 activities, and concerns what counts as 'engaging in' an activity. Let us take philosophy as an example. The claim is that nobody could understand philosophy who had not engaged in it. We must remember the nature of the distinction: White's argument is that even if you had never played cricket, never cooked, never played chess, never spoken a foreign language and never climbed a mountain, he could give you some reasonable idea of what these activities involved by explanation in everyday language, possibly with the help of films, gestures and so on. And this is obviously true.

Now why cannot I do this with philosophy? I confess that my immediate reaction is not only that I can, but that it is precisely what I am supposed to do when I give my first philosophy lecture to a group of students who have never come across philosophy before. But the key to this mystery and the resolution of this apparent conflict of opinion lies in White's point that in the case of something like philosophy explanation inevitably turns into doing. Thus, seeking to explain philosophy to novices, I may want to say that philosophers are much concerned with conceptual analysis. But that will not mean anything to the students, so I explain it by example. 'Look here,' I say, 'suppose that somebody advocates "creativity" as an educational objective. Now the philosopher wants to know what counts as being creative. Is it enough just to produce something? Must what is produced be of good quality?' And before I know where I am, I am doing philosophy. Provided that my audience understand what I am saying, they too are philosophising. At the end of the lecture they do have some understanding of what philosophy is, but that is only because they have engaged in some philosophy.

I am prepared to accept this as sufficient argument to establish the claim that technically one cannot understand philosophy without engaging in it. (One might well quibble: is listening to someone philosophising, even with understanding, really doing philosophy? But let this pass.) Even so it does not seem to me to amount to the significant point that White obviously thinks that it is. All that is actually being said is that what one might loosely call 'explanation' will, in some cases, technically become 'explanation by illustration' and hence 'doing'; in addition where the activity involved may proceed as a purely mental activity, those who observe somebody engaging in this mental activity and understand it, may be said to be engaging in it also. Thus all we are really saying is that some activities are considerably more complex than others, some may proceed as purely mental activities, some not, and some are both complex and mental activities.

What is the upshot of all this? In practical terms it is not very clear. White's argument was designed to show that, on the assumption that ideally we would like to place all individuals in a position to make informed choices about what they want to do, there are certain activities into which we will have to initiate them. Most activities however can be readily explained to them, and that will be sufficient for them to know whether they want to do them. The trouble is that explanation will not be enough, if our object is to put them in a position to know whether they would enjoy engaging in a particular activity, and that it is not clear why it should take appreciably longer to *do* philosophy than to *explain* a Category 2 activity such as the social sciences. There is something very unsatisfactory about moving from the claim that philosophy has to be 'done' (involving an individual in listening to or reading introductions to philosophy), to the conclusion that it therefore needs to be part of a compulsory curriculum, whereas the social sciences do not need to be so pursued, because they can be explained. Even to be as well informed about the nature of the social sciences as about the nature of philosophy (as opposed to being in a position to know whether one would enjoy doing it) would surely take as long a time and demand the guidance of an expert.

Communication and appreciating art are perhaps odd men out in this matter. You clearly could not explain what communication was to someone who could not communicate, since explanation is a part of communication. On the other hand it is not clear what communication as a timetabled activity would involve. 'Appreciating art' stands out, I think, because the ambiguity of the phrase 'understanding what it is to want X' is in this case removed: the fact that we are unambiguously talking about *appreciating* art makes it clear that, here at least, White means understanding or knowing the pleasure that can be had from an activity. He is obviously correct that you cannot explain what appreciating art is like to those who do not appreciate it (though you obviously can explain the sort of things that those who appreciate art are appreciating). But then no more can you explain what enjoying playing cricket is like to those who do not play it.

My conclusion is that White's attempt at the systematic categorisation of activities does not work. At the same time, on a more mundane but not necessarily less important level, he is surely right that some activities are infinitely more complex than others, and, although understanding what is involved in an activity is not a sufficient condition of having a true idea of whether one would enjoy doing it, it is a necessary condition of being able to choose to do it. He is also correct in the general observation that with some activities, such as cricket, knowing what they involve is a more helpful guide to having an accurate idea of whether one would enjoy doing them than with others. If I dislike all organised games I have played, then an account of cricket as an organised game is likely to be enough to warn me off. But this observation cannot be categorically categorised: I might have enjoyed cricket if coerced into actually playing it.

VIII CONCLUSION

In this chapter I have tried to suggest that none of the curriculum theories examined, which I regard as a representative cross-section of all the types of theory most deserving of attention, are entirely satisfactory. But the shortcomings are often of quite different kinds. Nisbet's utilisation of subjects to meet objectives raises questions about his objectives and offers no particular reason to teach one subject rather than another. Perhaps there is no reason to teach, say, history rather than typing, but one feels that his approach is inadequate because it leaves out of account what might be distinctive features inherent in various subjects. The intuitive theory that there just are some self-evidently worthwhile activities is inadequate, because it is not an argument at all, but an assertion of belief – unhelpful, if only because intuitions as to what is worthwhile vary. Bantock's specific claims for the study of literature do not appear to be sufficiently worked out. Peters's transcendental argument does not establish that various theoretical pursuits just are worthwhile.

Hirst's categorisation of forms of knowledge does not square with his own criteria: there simply are not eight logically distinct kinds of proposition, each of which has to be assessed by different kinds of truth criteria. The claim that whatever a child wants to do is *ipso facto* worthwhile is implausible, and the related claim that children generally want to do worthwhile things (or that they grow to live worthwhile lives automatically) lacks any evidence to support it. Goodman's specific version of such a theory reads more like a utopian novel than a piece of serious argument. The hidden culture curriculum theory seems rather confused and does not offer any obvious reason to accept the conclusion that there is an identifiable working-class culture that ought to provide the content for the curriculum.

John White's attempt to divide activities exhaustively into two categories is unconvincing.

On the positive side White's observations about the need to provide individuals with the wherewithal to make meaningful choices, and the principle that some activities are more difficult to understand than others, may prove important. Similarly with Dearden's suggestion that the forms of knowledge, such as they are, should be introduced to children to facilitate their ultimate freedom of choice. In the final chapter I shall argue for an introduction to the two forms of knowledge, the two types of interpretative attitude, and the four kinds of awareness, as a necessary means to enabling the individual to exercise choice. But my argument for seeing education partly as a means to providing opportunities for meaningful choice will not be based on the value of autonomy or freedom. Rather it will be geared to a utilitarian touchstone. I therefore now turn to an attempt to present the thesis that a worthwhile activity is one that is productive of pleasure.

Notes and references

1 S. Nisbet, *Purpose in the Curriculum* (University of London Press, 1957). Nisbet's handy little volume provides a useful introduction to the problem of selecting curriculum content, taken on its own terms at a less than philosophical level. Ch. 1 outines both the case for some 'practical objectives' and the proposed objectives themselves. Chs 2 and 3 offer a more detailed account of the objectives. Chs 4 and 5 contain a critique of the various elements in the conventional curriculum by reference to the objectives. Concluding chapters look briefly at possible objections to the approach adopted and prepare the way for a more philosophical enquiry.

2 Ibid., pp. 98, 99.

3 B. S. Bloom (ed.), *Taxonomy of Educational Obectives: the Classification of Educational Goals*, Handbook 1: *The Cognitive Domain* and Handbook 2: *The Affective Domain* (David McKay & Co., 1956, 1964). This is not the place to embark upon a full-scale philosophical critique of Bloom's *Taxonomy*, with which I imagine many readers will be familiar. Bloom's fundamental concern is to isolate skills and attributes that can be *measured*. That concern, no doubt quite proper in itself and potentially useful, is to be distinguished from a concern to evaluate various skills, attributes, etc. or to consider which of them are valuable. Bloom and I are, so to speak, playing different ballgames. Nonetheless Bloom's activity does give rise to certain questions typical of my activity. For example: in the taxonomy, under the broad objective 'knowledge of specifics', we have the more specific objective 'knowledge of specific facts' (e.g. dates, events, persons). An illustrative educational objective is then given: 'The recall of major facts about particular cultures.' Similarly, in the affective domain, as an illustrative educational objective related to 'commitment' we find: 'devotion to those ideas and ideals which are the foundation of democracy'. Such objectives clearly raise such crucial questions as: How do you tell whether an individual has

such devotion? What counts as 'devotion'? Is the 'recall of major facts' a desirable or worthwhile objective? Do we accept without question the desirability of striving for 'devotion to the ideals of democracy'?

4 Herbert Spencer (1820–1903), *Education* (Watts & Co., 1929). Ch. 1 is entitled 'What knowledge is most worthwhile?' Spencer's answer, no doubt influenced to some extent by the impact of Darwin and some of the cruder forms of utilitarianism prevalent during his life, is, in essence, scientific knowledge. At the time of going to press certain utterances from Lord Crowther-Hunt suggest that we are about to embark on a new era of such short-sighted utilitarianism as that espoused by Spencer (for all that he asked the right question). One of the main purposes of this essay is to indicate that a proper understanding of utilitarianism does *not* lead to the advocacy of an education geared to social demands in the technological sphere. See Chapter 4. On Spencer, see A. Low-Beer, *Spencer* (Collier-Macmillan, 1969).

5 G. H. Bantock, *Education in an Industrial Society* (Faber, 1963), p. 94, footnote. Two of the main themes running through Bantock's various published works are: (1) the need to maintain high cultural standards, and (2) the need to keep political considerations out of educational debate. He has also devoted some attention to the problem of finding an alternative popular education for the many who, it is felt, can neither cope with nor benefit from an education cognitively biased. His themes obviously invite a number of questions and his writings have provoked some strong reactions. The distressing tendency for educationalists to become polarised in a 'progressive left wing' or 'traditionalist right wing' camp, coupled with the fact that he has contributed to the Black Papers, has probably led to a rather unsubtle classification of Bantock in some quarters. While I find his forays into the realm of a theory of popular education weak, and while I disagree with much of what he has to say on other aspects of education, Bantock remains, in my view, an author well worth reading.

6 R. S. Peters, whether one likes it or not, is, at the time of writing, still without question the most influential figure in the philosophy of education in this country. There are signs that some people evidently do not like it (see, for instance, D. Adelstein, ' "The Philosophy of Education" or the Wisdom and Wit of R. S. Peters', in T. Pateman (ed.), *Counter Course*, Penguin, 1972; *The Great Brain Robbery*, Moss Side Press Ltd; and H. Bowden, 'On the Selection, Organisation and Assessment of Knowledge for Teachers', in *Education for Teaching*, Autumn, 1972). As with Bantock, although I do not agree with some of what Peters has to say, I regard his work as being of considerable interest and importance. Certainly most of his critics fail to measure up to him. *Ethics and Education* (George Allen & Unwin, 1966) remains the best comprehensive introduction to his work. On Peters and the Transcendental argument, see J. R. Kleinig, 'R. S. Peters' Use of Transcendental Arguments', in *Proc. Phil. Ed. Soc. G.B.*, 1973, vol. 7, no. 2, and J. P. White, *Towards a Compulsory Curriculum* (Routledge & Kegan Paul, 1973), chs 2 and 6.

7 P. H. Hirst, 'Liberal Education and the Nature of Knowledge', in R. D. Archambault (ed.), *Philosophical Analysis and Education* (Routledge & Kegan Paul, 1965). Hirst's paper has been variously reprinted, its most recent appearance being in P. H. Hirst, *Knowledge and the Curriculum* (Routledge & Kegan Paul, 1975). This collection of papers by Hirst also includes later emendations to the 'forms of knowledge' thesis and replies to certain criticisms.

8   P. H. Hirst, 'Forms of Knowledge Revisited', in *Knowledge and the Curriculum*, op. cit., p. 85.

9   P. H. Hirst, 'Liberal Education and the Nature of Knowledge', in *Knowledge and the Curriculum*, op. cit., p. 42.

10 R. F. Dearden, *The Philosophy of Primary Education* (Routledge & Kegan Paul, 1968), ch. 4.

11 P. H. Hirst, 'Forms of Knowledge Revisited', in *Knowledge and the Curriculum*, op. cit.

12 Ibid.

13 R. Barrow, *Moral Philosophy for Education* (George Allen & Unwin, 1975), ch. 11.

14 A. J. Watt, 'Forms of Knowledge and Norms of Rationality', in *Educational Philosophy and Theory*, vol. 6, no. 1, 1974, pp. 1–11.

15 The discussion on art as a form of knowledge goes further in, e.g., the Report of the ATCDE Conference on Philosophy and the Teaching of Art, held at the Madeley College of Education, July 1973, and in the interchange between Hirst, Reid and Scrimshaw in the *Cambridge Journal of Education*. These later developments are well worth pursuing, but they do not, I think, materially affect my comments in the text.

16 P. H. Phenix, *Realms of Meaning* (McGraw-Hall, 1964). The details of Phenix's account are not important for my present purpose, which is merely to stress that the accounts of Hirst and Phenix are not so much alternatives as different kinds of classification scheme, either or neither of which might be valid.

17 A. D. C. Peterson, *Arts and Science Sides in the Sixth Form*, Gulbenkian Foundation Report, Oxford University Department of Education, 1960, argues for four modes of human experience or thought: logical, empirical, moral and aesthetic. Hirst would appear to be offering the same kind of classification scheme as Peterson, but coming up with a more precise answer. The two are therefore strictly comparable, and must be seen as alternatives one of which is nearer the truth than the other. Whitfield refers to Hirst and Peterson in R. C. Whitfield (ed.), *Disciplines of the Curriculum*, op. cit., Introduction.

18 D. Warwick (ed.), *Integrated Studies in the Secondary School*, op. cit., p. 6.

19 R. C. Whitfield, op. cit., Introduction, p. 16.

20 Can Michelangelo's David be a proposition? I do not really see in what sense it could be, but it nonetheless seems possible that Hirst is suggesting that it might be. See above in the text.

21 e.g. P. H. Hirst and R. S. Peters, *The Logic of Education* (Routledge & Kegan Paul, 1970).

22 There are problems with this terminology, as there are with alternatives. At one stage I preferred the phrase 'activity-centred', but it was pointed out to me that the attempt to contrast 'child-centred' and 'activity-centred' might be misleading since an emphasis on 'activity' (in a different sense, no doubt) is characteristic of much child-centred theory. The danger of 'subject-centred' as a term is that it may lead the unwary to assume that all the curriculum approaches so far considered are concerned to teach subjects in the traditional manner. That that is not necessarily so should be clear from the discussion in the text of, e.g., Hirst. The approaches so far reviewed are subject-centred in the sense that they are concerned to locate some kind of content or subject matter that is worth teaching. That content need not necessarily and does not invariably consist of traditional subjects taught as separate entities.

23 P. S. Wilson, 'Child-Centred Education', in *Proc. Phil. Ed. Soc. G.B.*, Jan. 1969, p. 120. Although I shall not refer to him explicitly in the text, P. S. Wilson provides what is perhaps the most comprehensive attempt to explain and justify this kind of approach to the curriculum, especially in his *Interest and Discipline in Education* (Routledge & Kegan Paul, 1971). For a criticism of a central strand in his argument, see R. G. Woods and R. Barrow, *Introduction to the Philosophy of Education* (Methuen, 1975), ch. 7.

24 e.g. R. G. Woods and R. Barrow, *Introduction to the Philosophy of Education*, op. cit.

25 J. J. Rousseau, *Emile* (Everyman, trs. B. Foxley, 1972). For a general introduction to Rousseau's educational views, see also L. F. Claydon, *Rousseau* (Collier-Macmillan, 1969). For a critique of Rousseau's use of the term 'nature' see G. H. Bantock, 'Emile Reconsidered', in *Education and Values* (Faber, 1965), ch. 3.

26 Sophie, who stands as representative of the female sex as Emile does of the male sex, is to be brought up in a way that comes as a shock to those who have followed Rousseau's recommendations for the education of Emile. The following quotation gives a fair indication of Rousseau's view of woman's 'natural' role: 'A woman's education must therefore be planned in relation to man. To be pleasing in his sight, to win his respect and love, to train him in childhood, to tend him in manhood, to counsel and console, to make his life pleasant and happy, these are the duties of woman for all time, and this is what she should be taught while she is young' (Bk 5, p. 328).

27 A. S. Neill, *Summerhill* (Penguin, 1968), is probably the most readily available of Neill's published works.

28 In taking Paul Goodman as representative of a deschooling movement, I am of course doing less than justice to the subtleties and variations within the movement and to other prominent deschoolers such as Ivan Illich. Nor am I doing full justice to Goodman himself in concentrating on his paper 'Freedom and Learning' rather than on his various books, such as *Compulsory Miseducation* (Penguin, 1969). I have concentrated on the one paper because (1) it is readily accessible and readable, (2) it seems to me to contain reference to most of the key and contentious ideas behind the call for deschooling, and (3) I do not feel that any other deschooling literature adds any material or more persuasive points of argument. See P. Goodman, 'Freedom and Learning: the Need for Choice', *Saturday Review*, May 1968, reprinted in R. Hooper (ed.), *The Curriculum*, op. cit.

29 e.g. R. Hooper, op. cit., p. 107.

30 P. Goodman in R. Hooper (ed.), op. cit., p. 107.

31 Ibid., p. 110.

32 Ibid., p. 109.

33 Ibid., p. 111.

34 Ibid., p. 107.

35 Ibid., p. 107.

36 Thucydides, *History of the Peloponnesian War*, 2.41.

37 For further details concerning Greek education see R. Barrow, *Greek and Roman Education* (Macmillan, 1975).

38 P. Goodman in R. Hooper (ed.), op. cit., p. 108.

39 Ibid., p. 111.

40 As in my treatment of deschooling, so I have chosen to concentrate on one readily accessible paper for my discussion of 'the hidden culture theory'. For fuller, more discursive accounts of the sort of curriculum view I am concerned with in this section the reader is referred to various works of

C. Searle, B. Jackson and U. Keddie. The paper on which I concentrate in the text is: G. Murdoch, 'The Politics of Culture', in D. Holly (ed.), *Education or Domination?* (Arrow, 1974).

41   T. S. Eliot, *Notes towards the Definition of Culture* (Faber, 1962).

42   G. Murdoch, 'The Politics of Culture', op. cit.

43   Ibid., p. 90.

44   Ibid., p. 93. I am aware of course that the alternative definition of culture provided by Murdoch is not the product of some arbitrary whim of his. It is a standard sociological use of the term (see R. G. Woods and R. Barrow, *Introduction to the Philosophy of Education*, op. cit., ch. 9). My point is simply that there are two quite distinct uses of the term culture which are in no way mutually exclusive. It is no argument against those who espouse culture in some such sense as 'works of great artistic merit' to say that one is going to exclude that use of the term in favour of a sociological use. The following paradox in Murdoch's position may also be noted: the literary heritage kind of advertisement to which he takes great exception clearly wishes to suggest that what it has to offer is culture in the sense of 'works of great artistic merit'. But whether that is a valid claim or not, such advertisements and the way of life with which they are associated are clearly also examples of culture in the sociological sense that Murdoch is concerned with. In other words if our sole concern were to be with culture in Murdoch's sense, we should, amongst other things, be concerned with the book club world which Murdoch so evidently despises.

45   Ibid., p. 93 (see previous note).

46   Ibid., p. 95.

47   Ibid., p. 98.

48   Ibid., p. 96.

49   It may finally be remarked that even if my critical remarks are judged to be without force, and Murdoch's thesis substantially accepted, it is very difficult to see how that thesis could have any application to a great deal of potential curriculum content such as maths, science or French.

50   J. P. White, *Towards a Compulsory Curriculum* (Routledge and Kegan Paul, 1973), p. 18. The initial seeds of White's thesis are to be found in three articles that he wrote for *New Society* (2 May 1968, 6 March 1969, 30 April 1970). In K. Thompson and J. White, *Curriculum Development: a Dialogue* (Pitman, 1975), although the book was published after *Towards a Compulsory Curriculum*, we are provided with what look like exploratory interchanges between the two authors preceding the writing of the book published first.

51   Ibid., p. 22.

52   Ibid., p. 26.

53   Ibid., p. 26.

54   Ibid., p. 33.

55   Ibid., p. 33.

PART 2. A POSITIVE THEORY OF CURRICULUM

Chapter 3

A 'Worthwhile' Chapter

I J. P. WHITE'S ACCOUNT OF INTRINSIC VALUE

As we have seen, the basis for White's curriculum proposals is to be found in his view that individuals should be in a position to make meaningful choices between activities and life styles. Category 1 activities are not supposed to be more worthwhile in themselves than Category 2 activities. Rather the argument is that they are educationally worthwhile or that it is worthwhile to spend educational time on Category 1 activities, because they are the sort of activities about which meaningful choice can only be made after actual experience of engaging in them. His thesis as a whole is grounded on his belief that no activity can be shown to be intrinsically valuable for everyone. Nothing is inherently worthwhile but thinking makes it so – provided that the thinking in question is informed thinking. Consequently, even if we were to accept White's distinction between two types of activity, justification of his curricular proposals would be incomplete unless we also accepted what he has to say about intrinsic value. For, if one did not accept the latter, the way would be open for arguing that some Category 1 activities were valueless or that some Category 2 activities were inherently worthwhile. Conversely, of course, what White has to say about intrinsic value may be regarded as valid and important for curriculum planning, even by those who do not accept his category distinctions.

White begins by considering whether what is intrinsically good for a person is what he wants for its own sake. He concludes that it is not necessarily, since a person may want something for its own sake which is not good for him. 'A drunkard', he points out, 'who was playing with a knife and not wanting to commit suicide might have wanted to play with it for its own sake, but this could scarcely be considered intrinsically worthwhile if, on sobering up, he was grateful to us for taking it away from him.'[1] In other words there are situations in which, and occasions on which, a person might want to do something for its own sake, which even he would not regard as intrinsically worthwhile for him.

This leads White to hypothesise that 'what is intrinsically worthwhile is identifiable with what a person would on reflection want for its own sake'.[2] This hypothesis is accepted, once it has been explained that 'on reflection' is to be taken to imply that the person in question, (1) 'knows of all the other things which he might have preferred at that time', (2) 'has carefully considered priorities among these different choices' and, (3) *a fortiori*, does not make his choice when drunk, depressed, drugged, or in any other way suffering from a distorted outlook.

According to White, the qualifications implicit in the phrase 'on reflection' render his formula – what is intrinsically worthwhile is identifiable with what a person would on reflection want for its own sake – immune from the objection that might otherwise be raised: 'True, he wants X on reflection for its own sake, but is X really intrinsically worthwhile?' If a man, on reflection, realises that he finds everything except X loathsome, then, says White, it is difficult if not impossible to see what anyone could mean by asking whether X is really intrinsically worthwhile. 'How could it be', he asks, that anything other than the one thing the individual does not find loathsome 'could be intrinsically worthwhile for him?'[3]

White therefore concludes that, since what is intrinsically worthwhile is to be identified with what a person would on reflection want for its own sake, the notion of intrinsic value is something that is formal, ideal and subjective. It is formal in the sense that we cannot identify it with any particular pursuit or way of life: whether writing tragedies, say, is or is not worthwhile depends on whether an individual would on reflection want to write tragedies. It is ideal in the sense that in practice we may only be able to approximate to the conditions necessary to an informed assessment of whether a pursuit is worthwhile. In practice we are not likely to have knowledge of all available alternatives, for instance. It is subjective in the sense that what is intrinsically worthwhile may vary, since people may vary and intrinsic value is identifiable with their reflective choices.

That there is something offensive to common sense about this argument is surely clear from the conclusions that it necessarily leads to. For example it follows, as White is wise and brave enough to admit, that if people on reflection want to comb their hair all day until they die of starvation, then, *ipso facto*, that is a worthwhile way of life. And it follows that an activity may be regarded as intrinsically worthwhile one day and intrinsically worthless the next, even though the activity has in no way changed its nature. But precisely what is wrong with the argument is difficult to determine, largely, I think, because it is very difficult to determine precisely what White thinks he is doing.

Is he trying to ascertain what the phrase 'intrinsically worthwhile' means, is he trying to ascertain the criteria for the correct application of the term, is he trying to ascertain whether any activities are intrinsically worthwhile, or what? My suggestion is that, consciously or otherwise, he is running all such questions together as if they were synonymous, and that such a procedure is plainly illegitimate.

Perhaps it is true that part of what it means to assert that the life of reason is intrinsically worthwhile is that it is the sort of life that the speaker would on reflection want for its own sake, just as part of what it means to describe a book as first-rate is that the speaker rates it highly. But just as it is an entirely different question by what criteria the speaker rates the book highly, so it is an entirely different question by what criteria the individual selects the reflective life as one which he would on reflection want for its own sake.[4] There is then the third distinct question of whether some criteria that some individuals might appeal to, to explain their assessment of the reflective life as intrinsically worthwhile, might not be in some objective sense irrelevant or illegitimate, just as one might argue that to describe a book as first-rate because it is cheap is absurd.

Furthermore, so far as the meaning of intrinsically worthwhile goes, it is surely right to suggest that White's formula only gives us a part of its meaning. If something is intrinsically worthwhile for me, then it must be something that I would on reflection want for its own sake. But the reverse does not hold: I might on reflection want something for its own sake that even I do not regard as intrinsically worthwhile, for example eating sweets. On reflection, I want to eat sweets. Since I am aware that the consequences of eating sweets are likely to be at best negative, at worst bad, I can only assume that I want to eat sweets for its own sake. But I certainly do not regard it as intrinsically worthwhile. From this I conclude that intrinsically worthwhile is not identifiable with what a person would on reflection want for its own sake. It is a necessary but not a sufficient condition of an ascription of intrinsic value.

What, then, has White's argument established? To draw the conclusion that he wants to draw – namely that it is unacceptable to include some items in a curriculum on the grounds that they just are intrinsically valuable – he needs to establish that it is meaningless or plain false to claim that any pursuit is intrinsically valuable other than by the criterion that a particular individual would on reflection want to engage in it. That, I suggest, he does not establish.

When all is said and done, White has produced no argument at all to show that certain things such as science may not simply be intrinsically worthwhile, whatever particular individuals may feel about them. He has not shown that it is false, meaningless or absurd to assert that something like combing your hair all day is worthless, even if you would on reflection choose to do it for its own sake. He has merely arbitrarily ruled that kind of remark out as meaningless. Such a procedure is the more remarkable in that ordinary usage would seem to indicate that that kind of remark is frequent and taken to be meaningful, and yet White's analysis of the meaning of 'intrinsically worthwhile' seems to rest entirely on an appeal to ordinary usage.

There are two weaknesses in White's approach to this matter: his confusing the fact that something is not proven to be true with the assumption that it is false, and his frequent alternation between the phrases 'intrinsically worthwhile' and 'intrinsically worthwhile for him'. One may add that the latter phrase is itself ambiguous, since it may mean either 'as a matter of fact worthwhile for him to do' or 'worthwhile in his judgement'. This confusion is very apparent in the final stages of the argument: the suggestion that, if a person loathes everything except X, it is difficult to make sense of the claim that A, B or C are worthwhile for him, is taken by White to show that the question 'But is X nonetheless worthwhile?' is meaningless. But it does not show this. Perhaps it would be meaningless to ask 'But is X nonetheless worthwhile for him?', especially if that is interpreted to mean 'worthwhile in his judgement'. But clearly 'Is X worthwhile?' is a different question to 'Is X worthwhile for him?' One may consistently claim that a pursuit is intrinsically worthwhile, but not worthwhile for a particular individual in particular circumstances.

White has seen, rightly in my view, that the transcendental argument does not prove that, for example, philosophy just is a worthwhile pursuit, and he adds that he knows of no arguments that will prove such claims to be true. We may say therefore that the attempted proofs have failed. But White seems to assume, from that point on, that it cannot make sense to claim, or be the case, that philosophy or anything else just is worthwhile. In other words he moves from 'proof failed' to 'claim false' without a pause. But this clearly will not do: nobody has proved the existence of God or the truth of fundamental moral axioms. This may be, as some would maintain, because there is no God and there are no fundamental moral truths. But such a view is not necessarily entailed in the lack of convincing proof. One might equally well argue that, since nobody has proved that God does not exist, it follows that the claim must be false and he therefore does exist. The fact that we cannot satisfactorily prove something to be true does not necessarily in itself prove that it is false. Thus it might be that philosophy just is an activity worth engaging in, but that the only way of seeing this is by intuition. (The intuitionist view is of no practical help, as we have already seen, but I am only concerned here to point out that White is not entitled to assume that, if something cannot be proved, it must be false.)

Because he takes it for granted that a judgement as to the worthwhileness of a pursuit is a subjective matter, White moves easily into identifying 'what is worthwhile' with 'what is worthwhile for him', again begging one of the questions at issue. And now that this identification is made, he runs the question of meaning together with the question of criteria for use of a term, and effectively concludes that because the meaning of 'worthwhile' is, at least partly, something like 'commendable' there are no particular criteria for its use.

In all of this he may be correct, but there is no argument for the conclusion and no obvious reason to accept it. Against it are the consequences of accepting the conclusion. Is what I really regard as worthwhile – in White's terms, what I would on reflection want for its own sake – necessarily in fact worthwhile? I would rather say that the question is still wide open. White has said nothing to show that it would be odd for me to say 'I know that you are a strange beast who would on reflection want to sit around combing your hair all day for its own sake, but just combing your hair all day is not worthwhile'. Yet, if what he has to say about the concept of worthwhileness is all there is to be said, and if his conclusion is accepted, it would be logically odd to make such a remark. Since there is no reason to accept that it is logically odd, something must be wrong with White's argument.

It seems to me that, to resolve the question of what makes something worthwhile, a new hypothesis is required. Now, despite my criticism of White's account, it is possible that the hypothesis I am going to put forward represents a more detailed working out of his thesis, rather than something quite distinct from his view. For the hypothesis I shall put forward is a utilitarian one. And it is possible to argue that White is in fact committed to a utilitarian thesis, notwithstanding his claim that his fundamental value is autonomy. The basis for such an assertion would be, first, the strong link that he evidently sees between 'worthwhile' and 'wanting' (and the latter must have something to do with enjoyment or pleasure), and secondly his frequent references to 'harm' as a consideration that prevents us regarding something as worthwhile. Certainly one may say that White misleadingly fails to stress that, if what is worthwhile is identifiable with what a person would on reflection want for its own sake, and if one accepts a distributive principle of justice, it follows that one may make meaningful objective judgements about what pursuits are worthwhile in a community, from a community point of view.

Be that as it may, I shall now put forward the utilitarian hypothesis. My main concern is to make it quite clear what the utilitarian hypothesis involves so that the reader does not prejudge the claim I am making in the light of a conception of utilitarianism which, if it is not actually false, may nonetheless be different from mine.

II   THE MEANING OF UTILITARIANISM

First, let us clear away two basic and common misunderstandings. I am not using 'utilitarian' in the casual and general way that involves referring to any attempted justification of something as a means to some further end or any justification of something as being in some vague way 'useful', as utilitarian. Teaching the children of labourers the three Rs in order that they may serve as clerks, or giving children the necessary skills to become mechanics or pastrycooks, involve reference to utilitarian considerations in that loose sense of the term. But neither practice is necessarily to be justified by utilitarianism in my sense of the term. Nor is utilitarianism, as I understand it, to be identified with advocating that people should enjoy themselves on any terms. A school of happy children would not necessarily be justified by utilitarianism.

Utilitarianism, in the sense that I intend, is grounded on the premiss that what matters ideally is a world in which everyone is happy, that is to say a world in which people are not depressed, anxious, alienated, frustrated, burdened by a sense of guilt or inadequacy, bored, angry or, more generally, miserable. What matters in practice, therefore, is the attempt by a community to minimise such states of mind as these, which are logically incompatible with happiness, by such means as are available. The question of the moral acceptability of various possible means is likewise judged by reference to the ideal of happiness. The two most obvious and potent means of striving towards the ideal are the formulation of rules of conduct and the provision of a suitable education. Education should seek to develop individuals in such a way that they are in a position to gain happiness for themselves, while contributing to the happiness of others, in a social setting that is designed to maintain and promote the happiness of all so far as possible.

That there are problems in this thesis, some of which I have attempted to deal with elsewhere, I do not dispute.[5] But I suggest that the difficult and significant problems relate either to the question of proving the premiss or to the difficulty of achieving the ideal. In so far as that is so, the problems are not of immediate interest. I am not trying to prove the premiss; rather I am hoping to lead the reader to assent to it finally, when he has a full understanding of what it involves and leads to, and what it does not. Practical difficulties in the way of pursuing or achieving an ideal are of course quite irrelevant to the question of the validity of the ideal. It is true that 'ought' implies 'can', but when we say this we make a logical point to the effect that it does not make much sense to say things such as 'men ought to run on petrol', in view of the fact that men are by nature unable to do so. We cannot legitimately conclude from the dictum that 'ought' implies 'can' that it does not make sense to say that we ought to strive for an ideal that as a matter of fact we will not completely realise, or that as a matter of fact we sometimes will not know for certain how to set about realising. In practice, I have no doubt, we shall never completely attain to the utilitarian ideal. But there is no logical reason why we should not.

Perhaps the best way to expand and clarify what utilitarianism involves is to look at a fairly typical example of a misrepresentation of utilitarianism would in fact justify such a society. This it certainly would to MacIntyre's paper 'Against Utilitarianism', which is not recognisably against utilitarianism at all.[6] Rather it is against certain features of our society and our educational system which MacIntyre, rightly or wrongly, claims that people try to defend on utilitarian grounds. I must make it clear that I am not concerned to dispute MacIntyre's picture of our society, nor even his empirical claim that people attempt to justify such a society on utilitarian grounds. My objection is to the assumption that utilitarianism would in fact justify such a society. This is certainly would not do. If people, whoever 'people' are in this context, do make the attempt to justify the sort of society that MacIntyre claims we have on utilitarian grounds, then people are very foolish and evidently lack any real understanding of utilitarianism.

That this is so can be seen immediately from the picture that MacIntyre paints: how could a society in which students have nervous breakdowns because they do not know why they are studying whatever they are studying, in which people cannot find activities to engage in that are reasonable and satisfying to them, in which people recognise and resent hierarchy and inequality, in which 'feeling frustrated' and 'breaking out' are the poles between which people operate – how on earth could such a society be justified on utilitarian grounds? Yet that is the society that MacIntyre tells us of, and the society that he claims to be the product of utilitarianism.[7]

I repeat: this may be a fair picture of our society, and it may have arisen, as a matter of brute fact, as a result of people's attempts to be what they regard as utilitarian. But such a society certainly could not be the product of people who both understood and had the ability to achieve something approaching the utilitarian goal. These features of a society are not justified by utilitarianism. They are condemned by it. For the utilitarian goal is precisely one in which the pains of resentment, frustration, alienation and nervous breakdowns, as well as the more familiar physical pains, are excluded. On any analysis of that admittedly obscure and tricky concept 'happiness', such miseries as these are patently no part of it.

MacIntyre arrives at his surprising and false conclusion by an argument that contains three steps. We supinely accept utilitarianism, he claims, because we lack agreement on any absolute values. This is disastrous, he continues, because, since 'utilitarianism is necessarily interpreted in terms of the dominant beliefs and attitudes'[8] in a society, it justifies the *status quo*. Utilitarianism involves a view of education as something the nature of which is determined by extrinsic criteria, such as passing exams, getting a university place and getting a job. What we should advocate, he concludes, is a conception of education employing intrinsic criteria. We should consider education in its own character as the development of thinking or criticism.

Critical thought and the value of activities in themselves should be taught.

There is one point here that is of importance and is essentially correct, namely that 'utilitarianism is necessarily interpreted in terms of the dominant beliefs and attitudes' in a society. But the conclusion that the *status quo* is *ipso facto* justified by utilitarianism is false, as I shall shortly explain. For the rest, the argument is highly misleading. The first step is peculiar, to say the least. For since utilitarianism is based upon the notion that happiness or pleasure is the sole absolute value, MacIntyre's assertion seems to amount to saying that, because we lack agreement on absolute values, we agree on an absolute value. But in any case, since attempting to explain why people are drawn to utilitarianism does not help us in any way to assess the plausibility or validity of the utilitarian thesis, this step is in fact irrelevant to our present purposes.

The second claim, that utilitarianism necessarily justifies our present society, is false, as we have already seen, since by no stretch of the imagination could a utilitarian be satisfied with the present state of affairs, as depicted by MacIntyre.

The third point is of some interest. It will be noted that MacIntyre subscribes to the questionable view that there is a correct or proper conception of education, specifically that education is by definition about the development of thinking or criticism. Parallel to this view is Peters' similar view that it is some kind of logical or conceptual truth that the educated man should have cognitive perspective.[9] What is at issue here is not whether we do or do not agree that ideally we would like education to promote critical thought and cognitive perspective, but whether it is true to claim that there is some conceptual link between these qualities and education; whether, that is to say, education is by definition about developing such qualities, like it or not, rather as bachelors are unmarried, whether you like it or not.

My own view is that there are no reasonable grounds for making the claim that there is some kind of conceptual link between education and critical thought. It is just a fact that certain societies and individuals have not seen and do not see education in this way. On what grounds can we say that such people are using the term incorrectly? At best one might argue that there is a conceptual link between education and knowledge in a broad unspecified sense. This claim could be made to fit the facts, for, it could be argued, though the Spartans or the Australian aborigines offered a different kind of education both to each other and to us, all three were or are concerned with passing on to the young their knowledge. What changes from place to place and time to time, is the particular conception of knowledge. To the Spartans knowledge meant a limited amount of information and some specific skills. To Peters, and many others today, it involves cognitive perspective. But, even if we argue in this way, it does not automatically follow that we ought to be concerned to promote critical thought or cognitive perspective in children. Granted that we accept a conceptual link between knowledge and education, and granted that we accept that knowledge should be characterised not simply in terms of information, but in terms of something like cognitive perspective, we might nonetheless oppose the idea of promoting cognitive perspective in children. All we would need to do is say that we are not in favour of educating the young, now that we see what it means. We might say that we would rather train them, indoctrinate them, or leave them alone.

I am not advocating any of the last three alternatives. I am only concerned to point out that MacIntyre's implication that the development of critical thought is the proper business of education and ought to be our objective with children is an unargued assertion. Similarly, his demand that we teach children activities valuable in themselves presupposes that there are such activities, that they are identifiable, and that it is clear what it means to refer to an activity as valuable in itself. All of which, as we have seen, is, at least, contentious.

However a much more important point to note is that just as he interprets utilitarianism to justify what he pictures as a frenetic and depressing social situation, so MacIntyre assumes that utilitarians would approve of an educational system dominated by the demands of exams, which are in turn dominated by the demands of the universities and so on *ad infinitum* or 'to an end which never appears'.[10] And he also assumes that his preferred educational ends – the development of critical thought and the recognition of some activities as valuable in themselves– would and could not be justified by utilitarianism. My argument in the remaining pages of this essay is designed to show that precisely the opposite is true: that in the light of utilitarianism we can give some sense to the notion of intrinsically worthwhile activities, that as a result we can pick out some specific examples of intrinsically worthwhile activities, and that the exercise of critical thought is one such activity.

Before passing on to a more detailed description of utilitarianism, which will include taking due note of MacIntyre's point that 'utilitarianism is necessarily interpreted in the light of dominant beliefs and attitudes', it is worth remarking that his paper would constitute a reasonable case against utilitarianism in the loose sense of the term that we are not concerned with. But it is clear, from the references to Bentham and Mill, that it is supposed to constitute an attack on the ethical theory with which we are here concerned. It should by now be clear that it is by no means obviously any such thing.

The utilitarianism to be outlined is essentially that of Jeremy Bentham rather than that of John Stuart Mill.[11] The ideal is a world in which all are happy. I have already indicated something of what is meant by 'happy', by listing some of the states of mind that are incompatible with it. In positive terms, happiness is taken to be that feeling or state of mind which is dependent on pleasure or the satisfaction of desires. This is not to identify happiness and pleasure. And that is just as well, since clearly one can experience a pleasure without being happy. On the other hand one could hardly claim to be happy, if one took no pleasure in life. Happiness, conceived of ideally, is that state of mind that accompanies the satisfaction of all one's desires, whatever they are. Thus the completely happy man, whom we have to imagine, is one who has found a complete correlation between what he would on reflection, in White's sense of the term, want to do, experience and see about him, and what he does do, experience and see about him.

Such a man does not, so far as I know, exist, and we therefore tend to refer to ourselves and others as happy when, strictly speaking, we or they are only relatively happy – that is to say, when the desires that are dominant in us are satisfied to a significant degree, or when we take considerable pleasure in life. This indisputable point that none of us are completely happy has, I suggest, considerable bearing on the problem we often have in deciding whether we are happy or not. If we asked ourselves, as strictly speaking we should, whether we were fairly happy or fairly miserable, or more happy than we were a year ago, most of the alleged difficulties in recognising whether we are happy or not would disappear.

Whether this characterisation of happiness accords with that of the reader or of anyone else is, fortunately, an irrelevant question. This is what the utilitarian is talking about. I am not particularly concerned to offer a true analysis of the concept, whatever a true analysis would be. I only want to make it clear what sort of thing the utilitarian has in mind when he talks of promoting happiness. Thus the claim is, in Bentham's words, that 'pain and pleasure are our sovereign masters . . . it is for them alone to point out what we ought to do'. A person or community will be described as the more happy in so far as the aim of maximising pleasure and minimising pain is achieved. (But in practice, if the aim is achieved to any marked extent, the individual or community will be described simply as 'happy'.)[12]

Now come two crucial points. First, the utilitarian will accept a distributive principle of justice. The argument for so doing need not be rehearsed here, but what is involved is the assumption that if happiness is a good, then, *prima facie*, everybody should have this good. That convenient but, as it turned out, confusing slogan 'the greatest happiness of the greatest number' was designed to encapsulate this distributive principle coupled with a recognition of the practical difficulty of always ensuring that all gained equal happiness from some specific proposal. Because the formula has led some to postulate well-nigh absurd improbabilities about killing innocent scapegoats for the sake of the happiness of others, however, it is best to drop it. The aim of utilitarianism is to promote happiness, with equal concern for the happiness of all.

Secondly, Mill's attempt to argue that there is a distinction to be drawn between different qualities of pleasure cannot be accepted, since it is fatal to utilitarianism.[13] If it is true that some pleasures are better than others, regardless of the quantity of pleasure involved in either case, then it ceases to be true that pain and pleasure alone are our 'sovereign masters'. If Mill's claim is not actually rejected, then it must be interpreted as meaning that some pleasures, because they just are in the nature of things more pleasurable quantitatively, may come to be regarded as superior pleasures.

But basically we stick with Bentham's calculus. According to this, in estimating the quantity of pleasure arising out of some pursuit or activity, we have to take account of all people affected (the *extent* of the pleasure), the *intensity* and *duration* of the pleasure experienced, and the *fecundity* of the pleasure, by which Bentham meant its tendency to be followed by further pleasure. It must also be appreciated that *extent* of pleasure does not only refer to the pleasure that an agent's activity may directly give to others; it also refers to the pleasure that may arise indirectly out of an action or an activity. For example, a play may actively displease its audience, but it might implant an idea in the mind of one member of the audience that later bears fruit and brings considerable pleasure to many. Thus an activity may have instrumental value in bringing about pleasure, even if it gives no direct pleasure at all.

The last example was deliberately chosen for its lack of realism in practical terms. It makes the point about instrumental value well enough formally, but in this instance we have an example of something that we could not in practice assess. It is quite true that Bentham's calculus does not give us easy answers : it is not a ready reckoner. It is impossible for me to be certain about the degree of intensity of pleasure that you experience in watching a film. It is difficult to quantify extent of pleasure, impossible to weigh intensity against duration in any precise manner, and impossible to be certain that one action will in fact be more productive of pleasure than another.

If we were anywhere near the ideal of a happy world, then there would, I think, be some point in fretting over such considerations. But such considerations, relating to the difficulty of acting in accordance with utilitarianism, have no bearing on the question of whether we should be aiming for the utilitarian ideal. And since we are nowhere near that ideal, I see no point in fretting over such considerations. For surely it is quite unrealistic, even untrue, to pretend that, given what we know about ourselves – which might have been different, but is not – given the circumstances in which we find ourselves, and given the need to consider everybody, we cannot make significant progress towards the ideal. We can certainly do so, by aiming for rules, conditions of life, and activities the existence of which seems more likely to promote pleasure and diminish pain than their absence. This is what utilitarianism would have us do. And very often, in practice, there is no room for reasonable doubt that a rule or activity will promote pleasure.

Let us by all means acknowledge that, say, the question of whether there should be state subsidies to opera houses is not easy to resolve on utilitarian principles. But let us not pretend that there is any room for doubt that a rule against killing is justified on utilitarian principles, and let us not conclude that a theory is false or invalid because it is sometimes difficult to handle. (Besides, the question of state subsidies to opera houses is not easy to resolve on any ethical theory!)

I now return to MacIntyre's claim that 'utilitarianism is necessarily interpreted in the light of dominant beliefs and attitudes'. To some extent this is true. Utilitarianism must take account of such things, for people's beliefs and attitudes are obviously relevant to the pleasure that they will experience in various situations. It is also true that many different kinds of society might be justified on utilitarian terms, precisely because different groups of people may be markedly different in their outlook on life. (Perhaps, incidentally, this is a point in favour of the acceptance of utilitarianism, rather than a point against it.)

Many kinds, but not any kind of society might be justified by utilitarianism. What is not legitimate is to argue that any practice that currently gives a great deal of pleasure is *ipso facto* justified by utilitarianism. For it might be the case that ending the practice would, once people were acclimatised to the change, give *more* pleasure. Thus, even if we were to accept the questionable hypothesis that throwing Christians to the lions provided a preponderance of pleasure over pain in the Roman world (and assuming that the example were not already condemned by utilitarianism, since it offends the distributive principle of justice), it would not necessarily follow that the practice should continue. It would surely be reasonable to argue that a society which has eradicated the desire to find its pleasure in this pursuit, which is painful to many, gains more in terms of a balance of pleasure over pain than one which has not. This may be said without any specific quantification of the pain experienced by early Christians. One does not need to carry out literal measurements or prove anything. All one needs to do is appeal to common sense : more pleasure accrues to a society *in toto*, if the majority can find ways of amusing themselves that do not involve torturing the minority.

Still less is it legitimate to suppose that utilitarianism necessarily justifies the *status quo*. The answer to that claim is simple : if the *status quo* seems to provide the greatest amount of happiness it is practicably possible to achieve, fairly distributed amongst the population, then it is justified. If it does not, then it is not. The point is simply that it is true to say that utilitarianism is necessarily interpreted in the light of dominant beliefs and attitudes if 'interpreted in the light of' is taken to mean 'must take some account of'. It is false if that phrase is taken to mean 'must be dominated and dictated to by'.

III WHAT IS WORTHWHILE? THE UTILITARIAN THESIS

Just as my purpose in the previous section was to explain utilitarianism, rather than to justify it, so my purpose here is to explain what a utilitarian view involves in assessing whether an activity is worthwhile, rather than to demonstrate that we ought to accept that view. It is my belief that once the reader has a proper understanding of the view and of what does and does not follow from it, he will be inclined to assent to its truth, on the grounds that it is a more plausible thesis than any alternative.

The utilitarian claims that pleasure and pleasure alone has intrinsic value. This is *not* to say that any experience of pleasure is *ipso facto* valuable or desirable. It is to say that conceived of in isolation pleasure is a good, whether other things such as intelligence, friendship or aesthetic awareness, conceived of in isolation, are not good. They are not bad either; conceived of in isolation they are neutral, neither good nor bad. Conceived of realistically, as features of the actual world, intelligence, friendship and aesthetic awareness are good in so far as they are productive of pleasure, bad in so far as they are productive of pain. An experence of pleasure for the individual is good in so far as it promotes pleasure and/or no pain for others, bad in so far as it promotes pain for others.

An activity, pursuit or a way of life, then, is worthwhile in so far as it promotes pleasure and/or minimises pain. But, in assessing the degree of pleasure promoted, we have to take account of the extent, intensity, duration and fecundity of pleasure. Now, although the question of whether it is *true* that it is the degree of pleasure promoted that makes an activity worthwhile will not be answered by any mere appeal to linguistic usage, or by consideration of how such a thesis would square with our actual judgements as to what is worthwhile, it is nonetheless necessary to enquire whether this hypothesis fits the facts of our experience and our linguistic conventions.

This is an important point that deserves elaboration. We live in a philosophical climate in which some people actually seem to believe that one can draw practical conclusions from the mere analysis of how people use words. This, I maintain, is false. No fact about how people tend to employ the term 'worthwhile' – even if it were demonstrable, as it is not, that all people used the term according to exactly the same rules – would in itself establish what, if anything, *is* worthwhile in the sense of 'a thing that it is desirable for people to do, regardless of contingent beneficial consequences'.

If people were invariably to describe as worthwhile that which made them laugh, that which gave them intellectual stimulus, or simply that which they liked, this would not in itself show that such things *were* worthwhile in the sense of 'things that it is desirable that people should do'. Similarly the fact, if it were a fact, that all people regarded Shakespeare as an example of a playwright whom it was worthwhile to read would not in itself show that it was worthwhile to read him. What such considerations, if they accurately reported universal rules of employment of the term, might begin to do is make my sense of 'worthwhile' peculiar to me. Thus it might become apparent that when I ask 'What things are worthwhile?', meaning 'What things is it desirable that people should do?', I am confusing the issue by using a common word in an uncommon way. But that consideration cannot be used to stop me asking the question I am really interested in ('What things is it desirable that people should do?'), and that question cannot be answered merely by reference to how people use words or by reference to their actual values.

But, on the other hand, it is evident that, rightly or wrongly, if I produce a hypothesis as to the conditions on which an activity may correctly be described as worthwhile (in my sense), that significantly fails to square either with people's use of the term or their actual judgements as to what is worthwhile, then, as a matter of cold fact, people will not assent to my hypothesis. It is therefore important that my hypothesis should be seen at the outset to square, broadly speaking, with the way in which we judge things to be worthwhile.

If we accept the hypothesis, it follows however that the phrase 'intrinsically worthwhile' is misleading, since, strictly speaking, it is not true that something of worth inheres necessarily in the worthwhile activity. If, for example, we assume that aesthetic appreciation is inherently worthwhile, it seems, on this hypothesis, that what we would actually be saying is that aesthetic appreciation is valuable for the extrinsic reason that it provides pleasure. We talk about intrinsic value, but apparently mean extrinsic value. Is that not enough to damn the hypothesis?

Surely not, for this objection in fact applies to any view of what we refer to as intrinsic worth. When Bantock talks of the inherent worth of literature, he is obliged to make reference to the complex brain organisation needed to appreciate it.[14] When Peters talks of the inherent worth of certain theoretical pursuits he is obliged to refer to the effects, if not the consequences, of those pursuits.[15] The truth is that no credible theory could have it that activities carry 'worth' about with them, as purses carry money. When we call an activity intrinsically worthwhile we mean that it is worth doing even if it is not a passport to doing something else. But we can hardly mean that it is worth doing apart from its effect on us, or apart from the necessary consequences of doing it.

So, on our hypothesis, to refer to an activity as intrinsically worthwhile is to say that it is the kind of thing that, if done, promotes pleasure. What activities are objectively intrinsically worthwhile becomes now largely an empirical question. But, at any rate, in principle the hypothesis allows the legitimacy of making objectively valid judgements about what is worthwhile, which is an assumption of everyday talk amongst ordinary people, if not amongst philosophers. It also allows us to state categorically, although its truth is dependent on empirical considerations which I have not bothered to verify, that combing your hair all day is plainly not intrinsically worthwhile – which conclusion, I think, could not be more agreeable to common sense, ordinary linguistic usage and the facts of experience.

A crucial problem facing any theory that seeks to assert that some activities just are worthwhile and will necessarily remain so, whatever anybody happens to think about them, is the question of proof. As we have seen, none seems to work. Furthermore, it is difficult to believe that any activity could just be worthwhile in any circumstances. Nor can one forget that varying cultures have varying views of what is worthwhile. The hypothesis we are considering explains all this as nothing else can : for if we accept it, we see that there is truth and falsehood in this matter, there is room for objective judgement, but there is no eternal and necessary truth. At rock bottom what is worthwhile is a contingent matter. No activity just is and must be worthwhile for all time, for it is always conceivable that an activity that does as a matter of fact promote pleasure now might in the future cease to do so. Yet human nature in some respects seems relatively constant and so, despite differences between past and present generations, some judgements remain steady : some activities are as trivial to us as to our forefathers. Cultural differences are likewise explained : one might consistently maintain that in our society the study of literature just is a worthwhile activity, whereas in Eskimo society it may not be. (*Whether* it is worthwhile even in our society is a question I shall come to.) But though cultures may legitimately vary in their view of what is worthwhile, we can still, in some particular instances, meaningfully say that an activity that is thought to be worthwhile by an alien culture is not in fact worthwhile, even given their tastes, prejudices and way of life, because entire nations may conceivably be mistaken about what will promote their pleasure.

Another minor puzzlement of ordinary usage is that we tend on one occasion to refer to various activities as simply worthwhile or worthless, but on another to compare the relative degree of worthwhileness or worthlessness of the very activities that previously we described in absolute terms. If we can meaningfully ask whether we regard one or other of two worthwhile activities as more worthwhile, it seems that in fact judgements as to the worthwhileness of an activity are relative judgements. 'This is worthwhile' actually means 'this is particularly worthwhile' or 'it is worth doing this rather than not doing it' or 'this is more worth doing than a number of other things'. To describe an activity as worthwhile is not to ascribe some precise quantifiable quality to it, comparable to describing a figure as square or a man as six feet tall. The observation lends further credibility to the hypothesis, since, if worthwhileness is dependent on pleasure, it cannot be precisely quantifiable.

It should be stressed that the hypothesis says not that we *regard* things as worthwhile because they provide pleasure, but that they *are* worthwhile for that reason. But it is the totality of pleasure that counts and not simply the pleasure of the individual agent. Thus White is correct to say that the individual will regard as intrinsically worthwhile for himself what he would on reflection want.[16] But he is wrong to conclude that this assessment cannot be challenged or faulted: for what the individual would on reflection want is not necessarily what would as a matter of fact promote much pleasure *in toto*. If a man says that sticking knives in people is worthwhile because it gives him great pleasure, then, even if it is true that he would on reflection want to stick knives in people, we reply: it is worthwhile to you, but it is not in fact worthwhile. Your judgement that it is worthwhile, if that means more than that it is worthwhile as far as you are concerned, is just wrong.

I would claim, then, that this hypothesis not only fits the facts of our experience and our linguistic conventions, but also helps to explain them. But it may be felt that I have not faced up to the obvious challenge. Suppose that someone says that, when he claims that philosophy is intrinsically worthwhile, he neither *means* that he regards it as productive of pleasure nor in fact has he any reason to suppose that it is so. Let us call this man Ronald.

'Ronald,' say I, 'the first point is that I am not claiming that you consciously mean that philosophy is pleasurable, when you call it intrinsically worthwhile. You might, for all I know, mean virtually anything by the term "worthwhile", which is why I am suspicious of appeals to ordinary usage. But certainly, I imagine, in calling philosophy worthwhile you imply that you rate it highly as an activity. What I am interested in knowing is in virtue of what you rate it highly.'

'I just do rate it highly. Its value is self-evident to me.'

'But you would agree, being no mean philosopher yourself, that if that is all you have to say about it, you may as well say simply that you like it.'

'No. I like playing billiards, but I don't think of it as a particularly worthwhile pursuit. I may like philosophy too, but that is not why I value it.'

'But if you value this activity in preference to others, there must be something about this activity that distinguishes it from others in virtue of which you value it.'

'Not necessarily. Saying that it is worthwhile may be a way of reporting on myself, or may itself be the evincing of an attitude – rather like shouting "hurrah".'

'Well, that is a pretty unconvincing theory, since it is not what most of us think we are doing, and it would mean that some of the things we do and take seriously – such as arguing about whether philosophy is worthwhile – would be pointless. But if we are at cross purposes over a word, let me put the same question in a different form: is it correct to say that you think that, other things being equal, men are better employed philosophising than they would be combing their hair all day?'

Ronald paused. But he is an honest man, so he replied that it would be correct to say that that was his opinion. I asked him whether, in that case, there must not be some feature of philosophising that accounted for his regarding it as a superior kind of activity to combing one's hair. He agreed. The rest of the conversation is not worth reporting. Suffice it to say that he suggested a number of features, such as the intellectual nature of philosophising, but in each case he conceded that he had no argument to support his contention that the feature in question was valuable. He could not deny that it made perfectly good sense for me to say 'I know that philosophy is an intellectual activity, but why is intellectual activity valuable? Why is the fact that philosophy is an intellectual pursuit supposed to make it clear to me why you think it worth doing?'

My point, as against Ronald and, incidentally, G. E. Moore,[17] is that the only kind of reply that could have been given to my persistent questioning that would have made it silly for me to go on would have been one couched in terms of pleasure. If Ronald were to have said that he regarded philosophy as worthwhile because he enjoyed it, that would have put a stop to the conversation. For me to say 'I know that you enjoy it, but why do you think it worth doing?' would be as absurd as it is reasonable for me to say 'I know that it provides intellectual stimulation, but why do you think it worth doing?' This surely indicates that considerations of pleasure can stand as a sufficient reason for valuing an activity. That they are also necessary conditions can very easily be seen from the fact that, if we were to believe sincerely that philosophising must and could only contribute to misery, we should cease to regard it as intrinsically worthwhile. Is that not a fact?

So, I do not dispute that people value things that they have not assessed as contributing to pleasure and that may not in fact do so. I merely maintain that the only uncontentious reason for valuing something that can be put forward is that in some way it contributes to pleasure. This is not to say that a judgement as to the worthwhileness of an activity, backed by reference to pleasure, cannot be challenged. It can be, by disputing the empirical claim that the activity is productive of pleasure, by disputing that the pleasure arising from it is fairly distributed, or by maintaining that to refrain from the activity would produce a greater balance of pleasure, fairly distributed. Nor is it to pretend, which is certainly false, that nobody values activities that do not contribute to pleasure.

It merely amounts to saying that an activity that is markedly productive of pleasure is for that reason manifestly worth doing. Conversely, it does not cut much ice to maintain that an activity unproductive in terms of anybody's satisfaction is nonetheless worthwhile.

IV LITERATURE, BINGO AND THE EDUCATIONALLY WORTHWHILE

Now we are in a position to explain away the confusion surrounding pushpin and poetry, or, in modern terms, playing bingo and reading literature. Bentham did *not* say, as is commonly supposed, that from the utilitarian point of view pushpin was as good as poetry. He said that if the quantity of pleasure produced, taking everything into account, by pushpin were to be as great as that produced by poetry, it *would* be as good : an example of what those of us who had the good fortune to study Latin know as an open condition 'in which it is implied that the fulfilment of the condition is *possible but improbable*'. (I should say so.) For it would be absurd to maintain that in any society remotely resembling the complex industrial society with which we (and Bentham) are familiar, quantity of pleasure would be equal.

In the first place it is by no means certain that it is unreasonable to argue that, if an individual happened to be able to take pleasure in both bingo and literature, he would gain pleasure of greater *intensity* from literature. I stress this, because it seems to be too readily concluded from the fact that such a contention could not be proven to be indisputably true, that it is obviously false. But it might very well be true, and the fact that the vast majority of those who can do both with proficiency and pleasure feel it to be true may incline one to the view that it probably is true. Mill tried to use such an argument to establish that it certainly is true.[18] That, I think, will not do. But it surely is significant that, by and large, those people who can take pleasure in both, find literature ultimately more pleasurable (judged only from their own point of view).

However those who are unable to take any real pleasure in reading literature themselves cannot be expected to accept this argument. Therefore we turn to other considerations and take into account not only intensity of pleasure, but also duration, fecundity, and, most important of all, extent, including both direct and indirect consequences. With these considerations in mind, it is surely unreasonable to suggest that in so far as people who might have taken equal pleasure for themselves in playing bingo or reading literature as significant pastimes, devote themselves to the former, so far will the community gain in happiness overall. I do not say that in any conceivable society such a suggestion would be unreasonable, but that it would be in any society such as ours. Why?

Essentially because playing bingo has no further consequences beyond the immediate pleasure that playing it gives. True, the odd individual may win a lot of money; but for the majority when the game is over, that's it. There is not even much room for exciting discussion about the way the game went, as there is after a football match, since the game proceeds mechanically. Literature, on the other hand, clearly gains over bingo in terms of duration, fecundity and extent of pleasure. It has great instrumental value in terms of pleasure, since, by its nature, it has the potentiality to affect significant changes in the individual – in respect of his outlook, his insight, his perceptions, his ideas – which may have significant repercussions on the sum total of pleasure in the community. To put it very crudely: playing bingo necessitates and gives scope only for the capacities of an intelligent chimpanzee, reading literature demands rather more. People who are so constituted as to be unable to take pleasure in literature are, by definition, lacking in certain characteristics that are likely to be beneficial to the maintenance and promotion of happiness in a community such as ours.

It would be awkward, if I were misunderstood at this point. I am not so foolish as to maintain that those who enjoy literature are *ipso facto* greater contributors to the happiness of a community than those who play bingo. The literary pretensions of the Nazi hierarchy alone would be enough to ridicule that idea. And many lovers of literature, such as George Gissing and Baron Corvo, have been miserable old devils who never brought much joy to anyone by their lives.[19] But I do not need to make such an extravagant claim. Nor do I need to 'prove' anything.

All I need to do is to make two observations: (1) It is reasonable to regard the reading of literature as one intrinsically worthwhile activity on the utilitarian criterion. That is to say, it is reasonable to suppose that reading literature may promote much pleasure, directly and indirectly. (2) It is reasonable to suggest that the phenomenon of literature is likely to contribute more to the pleasure of the community as a whole than the phenomenon of bingo. This may be so, even if we concede that it may well be the case that some individuals are so constituted as not only to feel that playing bingo is more worthwhile for them personally, but also as to make it *true* that it is more worthwhile for them personally to play bingo. My claim would simply be that the community as a whole would suffer more, in the long run, given its broad nature, if it lost the sort of people who do take pleasure in literature than if it lost those who take pleasure in bingo.

In the same way, if we are to accept Mill's dictum that it is better to be a Socrates dissatisfied than a fool satisfied, this must be on the grounds that mankind ultimately gains more in happiness from the existence of a dissatisfied Socrates than a satisfied fool. Not, of course, a provable contention, but none the worse for that.

The point is simply this: if we had good reason to believe that the phenomenon of literature contributed in every way to man's misery, we should regard it as worthless. If we had good reason to feel that it contributed less to the ultimate and distant aim of achieving the ideal of a happy community than the phenomenon of bingo, we should regard it as less worthwhile than bingo.

In principle, then, activities can be ranked in order of worthwhileness according to their tendency to promote pleasure. In practice they cannot be so ranked with any degree of precision, because of the difficulties involved in calculation. We therefore confine ourselves, which is task enough, to picking out those activities which are manifestly singularly worthless and those which are particularly worthwhile. For the rest, not only do we not try to compare them, but we feel, rightly, that the very business of trying to promote the marginally more worthwhile at the expense of the slightly less worthwhile, would itself be a worthless activity: it would promote more pain than it would gain pleasure.

For example: Is theatre more worthwhile than television? Perhaps it is, perhaps it is not. Perhaps it depends on who you are and how you indulge in either. But one thing is certain: it would not be worthwhile to try and discourage people from watching television, even if there were reason to believe it to be less worthwhile than the theatre. Such an attempt would indubitably provoke more displeasure than would be gained by the outcome of the exercise. It is worthwhile in itself, which is to say particularly productive of pleasure, that over a vast range of activities people should be free to please themselves.

On the other hand we can assert categorically that making mud pies is a worthless sort of activity, whereas exercising reason is worthwhile. Making mud pies is worthless, that is notably lacking in pleasure potential, because we say – and I do not see why we should not say – that the pleasure to be gained from it is shallow and short. If this is not so in individual cases, we have good reason to worry about the likely contribution of the individuals in question to improving the lot of mankind. The activity contributes nothing to the pleasure of others, has no instrumental value in terms of pleasure, and, in short, has nothing to offer beyond that short and shallow sensation already referred to.

But reason has enormous instrumental value in respect of pleasure. Reason, of course, is no panacea. Reason may leave men cold or drive them mad. Depression may stalk contemplation. But such observations are nothing to the point, which is that only through reason can we reconcile differences painlessly, only through reason can we systematically attempt to promote pleasure and remove pain, and only through reason can we feel certain of proposed solutions to problems and new discoveries. Reason can be put to evil ends, but the exercise of reason is one necessary means to the realisation of the ideal of a happy community.

Thus MacIntyre was plainly wrong. No utilitarian, in the world as we know it, could be satisfied with an education that stifled critical thought. Things have gone too wrong, from the utilitarian point of view, for that. It is entirely reasonable to accept the proposition that critical thought will contribute more to the aim of promoting happiness than its absence would do.

It should finally be pointed out, although it has already been shown implicitly, that MacIntyre was wrong or misleading to claim that utilitarianism denies the value of activities in themselves. It denies that it is a necessary truth that certain activities are inherently valuable, but it nonetheless teaches that certain activities just are worthwhile at a given point in time, because they just do contribute greatly to pleasure. Listening to music just is a worthwhile pursuit, because it causes pleasure without pain, though it may be that it is not always worthwhile to sit and listen to music, or that it is not worthwhile to do it all the time. As against this, MacIntyre, and all those who maintain that some activities are necessarily intrinsically worthwhile, would seem to propose that some activities just are worthwhile, always were and always will be, and would be even if they could be shown to lead to universal misery. And this strange doctrine appears to be believed despite the fact that no reason can be given in support of the claim.

In the light of the above observations I turn now to education. Education is a process of development. When we set out to educate someone we take upon ourselves responsibility for their development. Whoever we are and regardless of how *laissez-faire* our attitude, we seek to superintend development in accordance with our view of what is worthwhile. But something that is not intrinsically worthwhile may nonetheless be educationally worthwhile. For a thing is educationally worthwhile if it is worth the while of the person being educated to engage in it, and obviously there may be some things that it is worthwhile for the child to do for extrinsic reasons – that is to say because they are necessary means to further activities, as learning to read is necessary to studying literature. Clearly what education has to do, from the utilitarian point of view, is to make a selection amongst possible activities, estimating worthwhileness by reference to the pleasure potential for the community as a whole of various activities. It then has to consider what activities or pursuits have extrinsic value as means to those worthwhile activities, and to seek to initiate children into those extrinsically valuable activities. Finally it must seek to develop in the child the capacity to take pleasure in those pursuits that are intrinsically worthwhile.

It is dangerous to say that education involves the initiation of children into worthwhile pursuits,[20] not because it is not true (it is), but because it obscures the absolutely crucial point that it is through education that

56863

pursuits can become truly worthwhile. To revert to the bingo/literature example: so long as people prefer bingo to literature we do face a genuine problem of calculation: we have to estimate the relative strength of the immediate personal pleasure derived from playing bingo, and the indirect extent of pleasure afforded as a result of people's studying literature. No easy task. But people are not born preferring bingo to literature. They come to prefer it largely as a result of their upbringing. The solution is obvious: bring them up to enjoy literature and there can be no question that it is a more worthwhile activity than bingo, since it *also* has instrumental value in terms of pleasure.

Here, I think, we have the answer to that peculiar fraternity which maintains that if the child enjoys doing X, it is not for us to say that Y is more worthwhile.[21] If teachers persist in this attitude, they contribute to making it true that X is more worthwhile, since the worthwhileness of Y is certainly diminished in so far as people do not enjoy Y. But such a policy is calculated to make the easy and the trivial as worthwhile as possible, and the complex and difficult as worthless as possible. And that policy cannot be worthwhile, unless we have reason to think that the community will gain in pleasure from a generation of people who delight in the easy and trivial.

Speaking broadly, then, education should seek to develop children in such a way that they acquire interests, characteristics and competences that enable them both to take pleasure in ways that do not harm others (ideally in ways that contribute to the pleasure of others as well) and also to contribute to the promotion of pleasure and the diminution of pain in general, by the way in which they behave and through the talents they possess.

In my final chapter I shall argue that a specific curriculum is demanded by such considerations.

Notes and references

1 J. P. White, *Towards a Compulsory Curriculum*, op. cit., p. 17.
2 Ibid., p. 18.
3 Ibid., p. 20.
4 On the distinction between meaning and criteria for use, see, e.g., R. G. Woods and R. Barrow, *Introduction to the Philosophy of Education*, op. cit., pp. 14–16, and J. Hospers, *An Introduction to Philosophical Analysis*, op. cit., ch. 1.
5 As explained in the Introduction, what I have tried to do here is give a brief and clear outline of utilitarianism without undue repetition of what I have written elsewhere. Those who are familiar with my *Plato, Utilitarianism and Education* (Routledge & Kegan Paul, 1975) and my *Moral Philosophy for*

Education (George Allen & Unwin, 1975) will nonetheless find some similarities between parts of this chapter and those books. Those not familiar with those books will find that the former concentrates largely on an attempt to analyse the concept of happiness and to justify the claim that the principle of happiness should override all other moral principles (chs 4, 5, 6 and 7). Ch. 6 of the latter book deals in a more general way with traditional objections to the utilitarian thesis, while ch. 11 provides the immediate taking off point for this essay.

6   A. MacIntyre, 'Against Utilitarianism', in T. Hollins (ed.), *Aims in Education: the Philosophic Approach* (Manchester University Press, 1964). The editor of the volume notes in his Introduction that, although the papers were not prepared around any central theme, every contributor nonetheless 'puts forward as his chief aim of education the development of rationality in children'. This certainly applies to MacIntyre. I argue in the text that there seems to be a confusion in MacIntyre's paper between 'utilitarian' in the vulgar sense and 'utilitarian' in the technical sense. But for those who are not familiar with the paper itself I may add here that the following seems a fair account of the substance of his argument. What MacIntyre is against is, in the words of J. Anderson which he quotes, that view of education which considers 'it in its contribution to something else, subordinating it in this way to the non-educational and running the greatest risk of distorting its character'. He is against teachers such as Dickens's Mr Gradgrind in *Hard Times*. He quite fairly points out that utilitarians such as Bentham and Mill no more wanted Gradgrinds than Dickens did, but adds the important qualification that 'what Gradgrind and Bounderby are is what utilitarianism *had to become* when embodied as a belief in the particular social structure which is early industrial capitalism. *Utilitarianism is necessarily interpreted in terms of the dominant beliefs and attitudes*' (my italics). I have dealt fully (in the text) with the important point made by the quotation in italics. Here I wish to stress that I too am against what MacIntyre is against. I too am in favour of developing the critical mind that MacIntyre is in favour of. Given that, I would feel somewhat guilty about making an issue of the fact that what MacIntyre seems to regard as a utilitarian education is not what I mean by it, were it not that my sole concern here is to bring out the distinction between a concern for utility in the vulgar sense and what I take to be implied by a serious commitment to the utilitarianism of Bentham. In short my use of MacIntyre's paper is more a device to bring out what I mean by utilitarianism than a serious attack on his stimulating paper. The only major point of deep-seated disagreement between us, I suspect, is that I do not think it is true that 'utilitarianism is necessarily interpreted in terms of the dominant beliefs and attitudes' in quite the sense that MacIntyre appears to think it is.

7   These examples and phrases are all taken from MacIntyre. They are dotted about in his paper and some come from other authors whom he quotes with approval.

8   A. MacIntyre, 'Against Utilitarianism', op. cit., p. 4.

9   See, e.g., R. S. Peters, *Ethics and Education*, op. cit., pt 1.

10   A. MacIntyre, op. cit., p. 17.

11   See especially J. Bentham, *The Principles of Morals and Legislation* (Hafner, 1948), chs 1–5. Although it is usual to cite Francis Hutcheson (1694–1747) as technically the founder of an explicit theory that became utilitarianism, Jeremy Bentham (1748–1832) may legitimately be seen as the effective founder. He was influenced by his friend James Mill, the father of John

Stuart Mill (1806–1873). The latter is probably the most well known of the utilitarians in the popular mind, if only because he was less of a recluse than Bentham and because such essays as his *Utilitarianism* and *On Liberty* are short and eminently readable.

12 These paragraphs on 'happiness' represent a shortened account of what I have to say in *Plato, Utilitarianism and Education*, op. cit., ch. 4.

13 J. S. Mill, *Utilitarianism*, ch. 2 (see M. Warnock (ed.), *J. S. Mill: Utilitarianism*, Fontana, 1962).

14 See above, Ch. 2.ii.

15 See above, Ch. 2.ii.

16 See above, Ch. 3.i.

17 G. E. Moore, *Principia Ethica* (Cambridge University Press, 1903), tried to argue against utilitarianism on the grounds that 'good' and 'pleasurable' could not be identified. His grounds were the claim that it always made sense to say of any particular pleasurable activity 'I know that this is productive of pleasure, but is it good?' There are two objections to Moore's argument: (1) Although we think that it would always make sense to ask that question, we might be wrong. It is conceivable that what is pleasurable is good, and that it is only because we do not realise this that we think Moore's question makes sense. (2) In any case utilitarianism does not claim that whatever is productive of pleasure is *ipso facto* wholly good or right. As I explain in the text, it holds that the only thing that is good in itself is pleasure, from which it only follows that something which is wholly productive of pleasure, taking everyone affected into account, is better than alternatives of which this is not so. Non-utilitarians will no doubt continue to dispute this. But there is clearly a difference between saying 'This gives me some pleasure, therefore it is good' and 'This, of the available alternatives, is the most productive of unalloyed pleasure for all concerned, therefore it is best'. The former remark might seem to be vulnerable to Moore's challenge; but it is the latter remark that more accurately represents the utilitarian view. As against Moore I am arguing, in the text, that pleasure constitutes an immediately comprehensible reason for approving something, in a way that nothing else does.

18 J. S. Mill, *Utilitarianism*, op. cit., ch. 2.

19 I cite the novelists George Gissing (d. 1903) and Frederick Rolfe, self-styled Baron Corvo (d. 1913), mainly because in their distinctive ways they were both unhappy men whose personal lives brought little joy to others. Gissing seems merely to have found it hard to find a social milieu in which he was wholly at ease and, at least until the end of his life, to form satisfactory relationships with the opposite sex. Corvo was simply embittered to the point of paranoia. But Gissing's *New Grub Street* and Corvo's *Hadrian the Seventh* might nonetheless be said to have made the manner of their existence worthwhile on utilitarian terms.

20 As does R. S. Peters, *Ethics and Education*, op. cit., pt 1.

21 See, e.g., P. S. Wilson, 'Child-Centred Education', op. cit., and above, Ch. 2.iv.

Chapter 4

The Curriculum

I INTRODUCTION

Having put forward and explained the hypothesis that associates the concept of the worthwhile with pleasure, how am I going to set about 'causing the reader's mind to assent to its truth'? I am going to outline a specific curriculum, putting forward my reasons for the inclusion of each element. In each case the reasoning ultimately relates to considerations of pleasure, although the precise nature of the link between the activity and pleasure varies considerably from element to element, and the manner in which I present my argument for each element varies accordingly. One hardly needs to do more than state that physical health is a means to gaining pleasure and avoiding pain, whereas the claim that it is worthwhile for children to study history, in the sense that such study is particularly conducive to maximising pleasure in the community, requires rather more explication.

My hope is that the reader will be convinced by the reasoning that this is indeed a worthwhile curriculum. Now part of my general claim is that the utilitarian account of how we are to estimate whether activities are worthwhile, if accepted, must lead to the advocacy of some such curriculum as this. If that is correct, and the reader feels that the curriculum presented is indeed worthwhile, that surely is a consideration to incline one to accept the truth of the hypothesis. It does not 'prove', in the sense of incontestably establish the truth of, the hypothesis. But it does provide a reason for assenting to its truth. And that reason is particularly strong if the criticisms of alternative theories in Chapter 2 are accepted. For, assuming that to be the case, we have a curriculum which we feel to be worthwhile, that cannot be *shown* to be worthwhile on any theory other than the utilitarian theory.

The curriculum is put forward as a practical ideal. It is not Utopian. It is ideal in the sense that to put it into practice would require certain changes in teachers' attitudes, teaching skills, parental attitudes, government directives and so on. But it is practical in the sense that these changes could easily come about. It is also ideal in the sense that the claims made for the curriculum involve what ideally would result from it. No doubt, in practice, like any other curriculum, it would not prove one hundred per cent effective even on its own terms.

More generally, I write, as one must, in the light of certain assumptions about the nature of our society. I do not assume that our society is the best in the best of all possible worlds, nor that it should not or will not change in various ways. But I do assume that we are talking about education in a society that will continue to be industrial, to necessitate living together in crowded conditions, to demand that people work for their living (some in relatively uncongenial jobs), to provide probably increased leisure time, and to be democratic in the sense that individuals have a more or less unlimited right to free speech and a say in electing their leaders. I also assume a society markedly dependent on such things as electricity, cinema, motor transport, etc. for its pleasure and containing within it a wide variety of attitudes and opinions.

One or two further observations need to be made prior to examining the proposed curriculum, if the recommendations are to be properly understood. First, following John White, I propose that a significant amount of time should be given over to a wide range of options, but there remains a hard core which is proposed as a compulsory curriculum for virtually all children.[1] (The exceptions would be those children who fall into clearly distinguishable categories such as the physically disabled and the educationally subnormal.) As White rightly points out, compulsion is not coercion. To argue for a compulsory curriculum is not to say that pupils must be bullied and threatened into activities. It is not in itself to say anything about how children should be treated. It will be remembered that throughout this essay my primary interest is in examining whether a case can be made for the desirability of any specific curriculum content. To propose a compulsory curriculum is merely to claim that there is a content which it is desirable to put before children and into which, by some means or other, provided that they are morally acceptable means, children should be initiated. If, when presented with a desirable curriculum, children will of their own accord opt to partake in it, well and good. To say that it is compulsory is to say that, if children will not as a matter of fact spontaneously choose it, they should be introduced to it nonetheless. The argument to justify such compulsion is to be found partly in the inadequacy of counter-arguments to the effect that children should be free to do what they want to do (see Chapter 2), and partly in the argument for the desirability of the curriculum itself: if I can convince the reader that it is desirable that children should pursue the curriculum I outline, it follows that we have good reason to restrict their freedom not to pursue it.

To this it should be added that to propose a common curriculum for all does not necessarily involve proposing a common teaching approach, or the assumption that all will make the same degree of progress in all aspects of the compulsory curriculum. It involves only the assumption that something of value may be gained by all children, by some means or other, from the curriculum. *A priori* I cannot see any reason to suppose that any child (with the exceptions noted above) could not cope adequately with the curriculum that I shall outline.

Secondly, it is absolutely imperative, if misunderstanding is to be avoided, that when I talk about 'history', 'social studies' or 'science', for example, the reader should note what I say I mean by these terms, and not judge what I say about history, social studies, etc. as if I were talking about what *he* means by the terms.

Thirdly, it may be noted that a curriculum must be assessed in the light of what is excluded as well as what is included, and consequently I shall have something to say later about those elements that are only optional, such as modern languages, and those that are excluded altogether, such as angling. Here I wish to note that an exclusion does not necessarily denote a judgement of worthlessness. This curriculum does not purport to represent an exhaustive collection of the most worthwhile pursuits. It purports to represent a hard core of pursuits that it is worthwhile that children should study. The claim is that it is more worthwhile that children should be initiated into the compulsory curriculum than that they should not be or than that they should be initiated into anything else. This is extremely important for understanding what follows. A number of things that I think are worthwhile, and which can be shown to be worthwhile in themselves on the utilitarian hypothesis, are nonetheless only optional; equally a number of things that are not worthwhile in themselves are compulsory. The key to understanding why this should be so is to remember the distinction between an activity being worthwhile and it being worthwhile for a particular person to participate in an activity at a particular time.

Finally, a word on 'intelligence' and 'transfer of training'. Anybody who is even slightly familiar with the study of education will know that the concept of 'intelligence' is extremely obscure. Different intelligence tests have clearly been attempting to measure different things, and it is very seldom made explicit what a particular theory or theorist means by the term. The result is that it is extremely difficult to be certain what, if anything, we know about intelligence. For that reason I shall avoid using the term.

So far as 'transfer of training' goes, I take it that there is no convincing evidence to support the suggestion that acquired competence in one sphere can as a general rule be transferred automatically to other spheres. Problem-solving ability in one area does not necessarily lead to problem-solving ability in another. Not only is there inadequate evidence for such a thesis, but it is *a priori* an unlikely thesis anyway, since the ability to solve problems in, or cope competently with, any one sphere clearly requires more than some general ability, even if there were such a factor as a general problem-solving ability. It requires, at least, interest, information and methodological know-how related to the sphere in question as well.

From this I conclude that arguments that make claims for a subject or discipline with respect to their propensity to provide a general intellectual ability or problem-solving capacity are at best likely to be misleading and, at worst, false. On the other hand attitudes and certain specific mental skills, I take it, are obviously transferable. Thus an attitude such as a *concern* for evidence may be transferred from one sphere to another, in a way that *ability* to cope with evidence in one sphere may not automatically be transferred to another sphere. The ability to memorise or calculate is transferable in a way that the ability to solve problems is not.

With these points in mind, I turn now to an outline of the curriculum.

The proposed curriculum falls into four stages. The primary stage involves health training, moral training, and the development of numeracy and literacy. The secondary stage involves initiation into the natural sciences, mathematics, the fine arts, history, literature and religion. The tertiary stage involves the continued study of history and literature and the introduction of vocational and social studies – all as compulsory elements. In addition it is at this stage that a wide variety of options, such as classics, cookery, carpentry, modern languages and the continued study of such things as mathematics, the fine arts and the natural sciences, are made available. The quaternary stage adds philosophy as a compulsory study to the continuing programme of the tertiary stage.

I do not intend to define these stages precisely, in view of the fact that determining when each stage should begin is dependent on empirical considerations of various sorts, besides which it is possible that the optimum point of time for one child may not be so for another. But, in broad terms, I am thinking of a primary stage lasting until the child is about nine or ten years old, a secondary stage that lasts for two years, a tertiary stage that lasts for three years, and a final stage of one or two years.

At any rate the reasons for the order of the stages are fairly straightforward: if a case can be made for health and moral training at all, it is clear that they should take place while the child is young. And since numeracy and literacy will be justified on the grounds that they are necessary means to various other pursuits, evidently they must precede those other pursuits. For reasons that will be explained, the secondary stage is concerned only to *initiate* children into the various elements listed. Since no great competence in the various subjects is purposed, two years should suffice to provide what is required: a realistic idea of what each one is about. This initiation obviously has to precede the tertiary stage, since the latter consists of options which include the elements from the secondary stage and the continued study of history and literature. Three years is deemed to be the sort of period necessary for converting the familiarity with the nature of the subject (history, literature and whatever subjects are continued as options) acquired in the secondary stage to a genuine competence in the sphere. The level of competence envisaged as the norm can hardly be quantified with precision, but I am thinking in terms of the sort of range of ability presumed in studies for the proposed examinations at sixteen-plus. Philosophy necessarily comes last, for the nature of the philosophical study I propose presupposes familiarity with other subjects and disciplines.

I shall now consider each of these elements in turn, explaining what I mean by each one, indicating the reasons for the precise status of each one where necessary (i.e. compulsory/optional/initiatory/recurrent etc.), and attempting to justify their inclusion in such a form. In broad terms, which may prove useful as a guide to the following pages, the argument is based on the following distinctions between pursuits, using 'pursuits' as the most suitable general term available to cover activities, subjects, studies, etc. It is not suggested that many, if any, pursuits fall neatly and exactly into only one of the following categories. The claim is only that some pursuits may be distinguished by the extent to which they essentially tend towards one of these categories:

1   Pursuits which have only extrinsic value or whose value lies in the fact that they are necessary means to other worthwhile pursuits. Pursuits of this nature, such as the acquisition of literacy, are confined in the main to the primary stage. It should be added that here, as in all the other categories below, an additional principle for curriculum selection is provided by complexity, or the criterion of the need for and efficacy of qualified guidance. Literacy is no more extrinsically valuable than the ability to hear or the ability to perform various motor-acts. But in most cases the latter arise spontaneously, whereas the former does not.

2   Pursuits whose worth resides in the consequences of their performance by some people for the community as a whole, rather than in any consequences of their performance for the agent, over and above the pleasure he may take in the performance. The last is discounted on the grounds that all the pursuits we are concerned with may prove pleasurable to the individual agent, but we have no way of knowing in advance whether in particular instances they will be so or not. An example of this type of pursuit, I shall argue, is

science, and such pursuits provide some of the elements into which the curriculum compulsorily initiates all.

3   The remaining pursuits into which the curriculum provides a compulsory initiation are understanding of the other types of awareness, besides the scientific. The relative worth of having some such understanding, it will be argued, lies partly in the range and ubiquity of pleasurable experiences to which it is a necessary means, and partly in the fact that it is also a necessary means to understanding the perspective or outlook of other people in certain situations.

4   Pursuits whose worth resides essentially in their advantage to the individual in conducting his daily life to his own satisfaction and the satisfaction of the rest of the community. Such pursuits form the core of the compulsory curriculum.

5   Pursuits which are relatively complex, but which we have reason to believe can be sources of considerable satisfaction to the agent and are, at worst, not inimical to the satisfaction of others. Pursuits of this kind constitute the list of options in the curriculum, though, for practical reasons, further criteria have to be brought into play to distinguish between the vast number of pursuits that come into this category, as will be explained in detail below.

II   PRIMARY STAGE

a.   *Health training and education*

Physical health is indisputably a *sine qua non* of most people's pleasure. Without it one is at worst dead, and at best denied access to certain activities. Without it one is liable to have direct immediate experience of pain and also to contribute to the pain of others either directly or indirectly. Direct pain to others may be occasioned by the fact that the sick person constitutes a burden to those around him in such ways as that he needs attention or fails to provide for them; indirect pain to the community at large is occasioned by the fact that the sick person draws on resources that might have been directed elsewhere, and in that he does not play a full part in contributing to the maintenance of society and the well-being of all. So much is obvious: the promotion of health is desirable in the interests of all. To the extent that health is attainable by effort it should be attained.

It is, therefore, a proper part of the educational process to ensure the healthy physical development of children and the maintenance of that health in so far as it is possible. That it seems entirely legitimate to refer to a man as 'educated' even though he is chronically sick, I do not dispute. I am making no conceptual claim here. I merely assert, with the confidence of common sense, that as educators we should be concerned with the promotion of health. This concern will in practice issue forth in two strands: first it will be our responsibility to see that children maintain their health as they grow, by ensuring that the conditions in which they live and work and the activities in which they engage are so organised as to contribute to that end. Thus, for example, an appropriate diet should be provided, and whatever forms and amount of exercise are deemed desirable by experts in these matters should be demanded by the curriculum. Secondly it must be our concern to inform children about physical health, about how to acquire it and maintain it. The guiding principle here, where we are concerned with education in matters of health rather than training a healthy body, should be the dissemination of sufficient understanding and information for the individual to be in a position to safeguard his health, rather than a concern to produce a deep and thorough understanding of human anatomy and the workings of the physical body.

I should add somewhere, so I will add here, that if it is true that it is possible to provide sex education that will contribute to a more satisfactory sex life for the individual and to the achievement of better sexual relationships (which I sometimes doubt), then, given the part that sex seems to play in some people's lives – given the potency of sex as a source of pleasure and pain – this too would constitute a proper element in a compulsory curriculum.

It must be admitted that such instruction, whether specifically in relation to sex or generally in relation to physical well-being, might in principle be provided by some agency other than the school. And, as I have already suggested, some might try to argue that sex and health instruction are all very well, but they are not part of what is meant by education. To this I reply that whether that claim is true or false does not much concern me, because labels do not much concern me. It matters little whether we call such activity educational or not. What is of importance is the claim that this is something that we ought to be concerned with in relation to children. The suggestion that the school should make it its business to see that such instruction takes place is based on the assumption that the school is an agency well suited to taking on this responsibility. My argument is simply that it is worth the while of the educational process to be concerned with such instruction, since it is contributory to the individual successfully engaging in activities that are in themselves worthwhile.

One point of detail: it is possible that the informative side of this programme, particularly in regard to sex, might be better postponed, or at any rate continued into the secondary stage. Whether that would be advisable or not is obviously a question that depends on empirical factors for its resolution and hence is no part of my immediate brief. My concern is limited to insisting that such health training and education should be part of the school's task.

Here, as so often, an important part of what I am saying is what I am not saying. I wish it to be understood that what I am not saying, I am not saying for the excellent reason that I repudiate it. Thus I reject most of the more fanciful claims made for PE sport and movement over the last incredible decade or so.

Some claims I reject because they seem to be plainly false. Renshaw is surely correct in arguing against Aspin's contention that 'moral principles . . . are actually part and parcel of the make up [of sport and games]', that 'moral principles, although central to *some* people's conception of what is entailed in playing a game, do not form a logically necessary feature of the notion of a game'.[2] If we feel moral outrage at the way a footballer behaves on the field, it is not because football is a species of moral activity. It is either because we feel that what he does is immoral in itself, regardless of football (i.e. he might punch up an opponent), or else it is because we think that a general moral rule is that people should abide by the (non-moral) rules of a game they are playing. There is really no good reason to regard sport and games as essentially moral activities, and no evidence to support the claim that moral attitudes that might be exhibited on the sports field, such as belief in following the rules of the game or in the spirit of team co-operation, will be transferred to real-life situations.

Similarly the view that sport and games are aesthetic activities and are therefore useful ways of cultivating an aesthetic sensibility, seems to rest on a confusion between what an activity essentially is and how one might choose to view it. Certainly one might look at a football match from an aesthetic point of view, but that is not what playing football is about, as any team that tried to concentrate on the beauty of its surge upfield would rapidly discover. In the case of some sports, such as figure-skating, it is very likely true that many of the spectators are primarily concerned with aesthetic satisfaction. But once again, even though a figure-skater could more reasonably concentrate on aesthetic considerations than a football team could, the activity of figure skating is a by-product of skating, and teaching children to skate is teaching children to skate. To teach children to sense an aesthetic dimension to figure-skating you have to do something related to sharpening aesthetic awareness, and you do not have to teach them to skate.

Some claims I reject because there does not appear to be any evidence to support them. As May points out: 'We have made comforting assumptions as to the creative value of dance and educational gymnastics. The theories have been well explored, literature on both content and method proliferates, yet little empirical evidence is to hand as to the

precise effects of all the various activities which are commonly prac-
tised at public expense throughout the country.'[3]

And some claims leave me cold because I find them incomprehensible
unless they are interpreted as relatively trivial statements stating simple
truths, in high-flown language, which do not appear to be particularly
important or to involve an adequate justification for putting the activity
in question in the curriculum. What, for instance, does the claim that
'the most important role [for PE] might be in the education of the
feelings and the senses and in achieving a high degree of self-knowledge'[4]
actually mean? What kind of self-knowledge that is particularly worth
having do I get from doing PE? What does 'Movement is capable of
conveying ideas, moods and attitudes'[5] mean, except that one may
spontaneously express one's mood by one's movement or that one may
simulate moods by gesture and movement in mime? So what? How on
earth could Bantock (of all people!) come to the conclusion that a
valid 'approach to consciousness and mind', in something approaching
Hirst's sense of a developed rational nind, 'is through body awareness'?[6]

I may be wrong, of course. My scepticism may be ill-founded. But
what is so depressing is that so much time and energy should be ex-
pended on contortionate attempts to justify physical activities as intellectually respectable, when there is no need to do so. To proceed as
if there were a need to do it, is to take a very dangerous step. For it
implies that one concedes that the school curriculum should be exclusively concerned with matters pertaining directly to cognitive development or, at best, cognitive and affective development. (But even
here 'affective development' seems generally to be conceived in narrow
terms as a kind of perceptual knowledge of oneself and others.) But
why accept the premiss? What better justification could one have for
introducing children to dance, athletics, swimming, football and so on,
than that such pursuits will keep them healthy, and may provide sources
of pleasure both for the present and the future? If by the way they find
a quicker route to 'knowing themselves' than Socrates did, so be it.

b. *Moral training*
I use the word 'training' rather than 'education' advisedly. I am not
here concerned with anything approaching an understanding of the
complexity of the nature of morality nor with any probing of principles,
which, following Peters,[7] we may take to be a distinguishing characteristic of education. By 'moral training' I mean causing young children to
behave in social rather than anti-social ways.

Neither the use of the word 'training' nor the use of the word 'causing' need imply a totally non-rational approach. No doubt even with

very young children one can give reasons for one's assertions and claims up to a point. One can, for instance, in trying to cause the child to refrain from kicking other children, point out that the practice hurts them and suggest that that constitutes a good reason for not doing it. But it is clear that with young children at least the reasoning has to stop somewhere: you cannot very profitably discuss the question of why one ought not to hurt people with a four-year-old. My claim here, therefore, is simply that a second compulsory element in the curriculum should be provided by the concern to promote social behaviour by whatever means are deemed to be themselves morally acceptable and efficacious.

When I refer to social rather than anti-social behaviour I do not mean that in my judgement any society is right to bring up its children to accept its norms, whatever they are. If the norms are pernicious, the promotion of them is pernicious. But the logically prior question of what norms a society should adopt is quite distinct from the question of whether such norms may be deliberately inculcated. I have argued elsewhere, consistently with my analysis of worthwhile in terms of pleasure, for a utilitarian system of ethics and cannot repeat those arguments here.[8] But in the light of that position it will be understood that what I am claiming here, in specific terms, is that an essential part of early education should be the active encouragement of activities and ways of behaving that are beneficial to others and the active discouragement of activities that are harmful to others either directly or indirectly, such as bullying, stealing, cheating or, more generally, dishonesty. It will be appreciated that, in the absence of any evidence to the contrary, I proceed here on the assumption that people are more likely to refrain from such behaviour, in the long term, if they are initially discouraged from so doing than if they are not.

Moral training is not envisaged as some kind of subject. What is referred to here is the responsibility of the school to promote, by its ethos, concern for other people and for the observance of certain rules of conduct. The justification for promoting such concern is once again the consideration that, if successful, it will lead to a situation in which people behave in ways that minimise pain in general.

I have argued on a number of occasions elsewhere that such a programme of moral training cannot legitimately be dismissed as indoctrination.[9] That is to say, you may call it by any nasty name you like, but there are no good grounds for maintaining that such a practice is morally objectionable. However it should be mentioned at this point that the curriculum does not involve confining the sphere of morality to this limited training. Far from it. As will become clear when philosophy is under consideration, in the final stage the child will come to examine for himself the very foundations of morality. But he cannot do that at the age of nine, and indeed he could not do that at any age, if he did not have any moral attitudes to examine.

More generally something approaching what most people would characterise as a genuine moral education will be provided through various aspects of the curriculum, in the secondary and tertiary stages. Information about people and society, awareness of a range of possible human emotions and feelings, and awareness of a variety of, perhaps conflicting, codes of value and preferred ways of life, which are surely necessary to autonomous moral decision making, will be provided. Concern for reason, concern and sympathy for other people, and the ability to reason will also be cultivated in so far as they can be.

The two points of importance here are : (1) The implicit rejection of any attempt to provide moral education by means of 'moral lessons' or time devoted specifically to moral issues – on the grounds that such moral discussion can only be meaningful in so far as the conditions in the previous paragraph are met, and might well prove to be counter-productive. (2) The claim that moral training should take place from an early age.

c. *Numeracy and literacy*
Numeracy and literacy are a necessary condition of the successful performance of certain tasks and activities, the inability to perform which would cause immediate pain. To put it at the lowest level : numeracy is a necessary condition of counting your change, which is a means to avoiding being shortchanged, which is a worthwhile objective since it saves you from a specific source of pain. Numeracy and literacy are also both necessary means to a variety of activities that may give pleasure in themselves such as the reading of literature, the study of history or philosophy, the practice of mathematics and physics. In itself this second consideration would not be sufficient to justify the inclusion of numeracy and literacy in a compulsory curriculum, since it still has to be shown that those pursuits to which they are a means are in some way worthwhile. But that I shall undertake to do below, and therefore for the moment we may justify the development of literacy and numeracy as having a small but not insignificant immediate value in themselves, and as being necessary conditions of engaging in a variety of activities which will be shown to be worthwhile.

Numeracy and literacy provide a particularly good example for stressing the limits of what I am saying. The fact that I refer to them as compulsory elements in the curriculum does not imply that they have to be imposed by traditional means without reference to the individual nature of the child. The fact that I place them in the primary stage does not imply that there are fixed ages by which predetermined degrees of proficiency should be reached. The claim is only that by about the age of nine or ten we should aim to have superintended the development of numeracy and literacy, by the most efficacious means available. Efficacious means are those that succeed in attaining the objective without promoting hostility to the activities in question.

d. *Summary of the primary stage*
So much I envisage for the basic minimum of the first stage of the curriculum. It is not a lot to ask, and hopefully it will strike the reader as beyond dispute. But it will be noted that, minimal and uncontentious as it may appear, it involves rejection of a number of educational proposals. Specifically it implicitly rejects the view that nothing should be done unless the child expresses an interest in it, the view that matters of health are outside the sphere of education, that the child should be left to find his own morality from the start, and that children should not be taught to read. To each of these proposals the reply is, in effect, that not to be concerned about the four elements that I have listed in the first stage is to act in a way likely to diminish the opportunity for pleasure and to increase the opportunities for pain, both as far as the individual himself is concerned and as far as the community as a whole is concerned.

I repeat that my purpose is limited here. I am not talking about methodology. I am not commenting on such issues as so-called creative activities, the desirability of field trips, topics for consideration or problem-solving exercises, or the need to develop self-discipline. I am merely suggesting, firmly and succinctly, that in the early years of schooling we ought at least to aim to ensure that all children are basically numerate, literate and healthy and that they have some concern for behaving in ways that do not cause pain to others.

With that in mind we can turn now to the more disputed area of the secondary stage of the curriculum, beginning with an examination of the natural sciences.

III   SECONDARY STAGE

a. *Natural sciences*
Under the heading natural sciences I include the study of physics, chemistry and biology. Now why should anyone regard such studies as worthwhile? I am not at this stage asking why anyone should value them as part of the school curriculum, but why anyone should value them at all.

Many answers have been given to such a question, but one, I should have thought, stands out as obvious and uncontentious. The natural sciences are valuable to us because they deliver the goods. They make an enormous contribution to our understanding and control of the physical world. We benefit from advances in the natural sciences in countless ways. Without such advances we should still regard the world as flat and the sun as the size of a moderate stone. With such advances and the application of increased understanding we have moved a considerable way to mastering our environment to our advantage. It is fundamentally to the natural sciences that we owe everything from television to electric toothbrushes. Our health, comfort, and opportunities to engage in a host of activities are grounded in the natural sciences. No other body of knowledge has such obvious utility.

It is true that without advances in the natural sciences we should not have had bombs, traffic fumes and revolting synthetic foods either. But the fact that our increased knowledge in this sphere can be put to bad as well as good uses can hardly be counted against the natural sciences themselves. They have given, and no doubt will continue to give us, the potential to improve our way of life from a material point of view. What we make of that potential is another matter. Nor should the fact that some may look nostalgically back on pre-industrial society blind us to the indisputable fact that our potential for combating such problems as disease, poverty and crowded living conditions just is greater. Furthermore, if we are to be realistic, although some may look back with longing to a way of life that vanished with the advance of industrialisation, it is most implausible to suggest that people as a whole would look kindly on a return to that way of life, if it meant the removal of all the conveniences to which they have become accustomed. (Besides, such nostalgic backward glances are pretty unhistorical: there is no reason to assume that life for the majority of people was more pleasant four hundred years ago than today.) Certainly it may be argued, to quote Isaiah Berlin, that 'the applications of modern science ... have increased oppression, danger, misery in some spheres, as well as vastly diminished them in others'. But 'the only real remedy for the evil consequences, whether of ignorance or of knowledge, is more knowledge'.[10]

So much for one argument, which is surely sufficient to establish that it is worthwhile to us that the natural sciences should continue to be studied. It is certainly worthwhile that there should be natural scientists, but what of the entirely separate claim that it is worthwhile for the individual to study natural science?

I shall begin by examining an argument designed to show that 'the curriculum of the secondary school should be predominantly, if not exclusively, concerned with science studies'.[11] This argument is introduced, though not endorsed, by Nidditch in his paper 'Philosophy of Education and the Place of Science in the Curriculum'. It is based on an analogy with Tudor and Stuart times when classical studies dominated the curriculum.

A classical curriculum, supplemented by Biblical study, was justified at that time, runs the argument, because the prevailing ethos of the time was a Christian neo-classicism. Three benefits accrued from the uniform adoption of a classical curriculum: 'One was the provision and per-petuation of a *common* cultural environment, frame of reference and store. Another was the intensive educational coherence at each stage, and through all stages, of school life . . . And third the content of what was studied had an international standing as being matter and manner that were normative and useful for all civilised and Christian people everywhere.'[12] In plain words, the fact that the study of classics and the Bible was the essence of all schooling, ensured the acquisition of a similar outlook, of similar taste and of similar values by all students, and imparted a unity to the various stages of education. The outlook, taste and values acquired met with the approval of people similarly educated and of similar outlook in countries throughout the world.

In addition, it was felt that as a result of his grounding and training in the classics, the student would be prepared 'in respect of language, method and content' for proceeding to study for one of the professions such as law or medicine, provided that his schooling was first rounded off by the study of logic, metaphysics and rhetoric. Such study occupied the first years at the university and was, of course, pursued by way of the classical authors. That this education had something to be said for it, regardless of the value of an intimate knowledge of the classics them-selves, 'is evidenced by the fact that the grammar school was the nursery of a crowd of distinguished men of letters and the learned arts, including Sidney, Marlowe, Shakespeare, Ben Jonson, Milton, John Wallis, Locke, [and] Newton'.[13]

By analogy, since we live in the Age of Science, rather than in an age of Christian neo-classicism, 'the curriculum of the secondary . . . school should be constituted by science studies'. A curriculum more or less exclusively devoted to the sciences, universally adopted, would pro-vide a coherence to schooling and a common outlook. 'The content of what would thus be studied has an international standing as matter and method that is normative and useful for civilisation and social develop-ment everywhere. The doctrines and ethos of Christianity would be replaced by the teachings and implications of science and by humanly determined values for personal conduct and for relations *inter vivos*.'[14] With the addition of some study of logic, as in the classical model except that modern rather than Aristotelian logic would be prescribed, the student would have been prepared 'in respect of critical-mindedness, method and content, to tackle properly and beneficially any subject to which he devotes himself'.[15]

As it stands this argument for a science-dominated curriculum will not do at all. (Since I have quoted extensively from Nidditch, I must repeat that he does not endorse this argument. His real attitude to it has to be gauged from his ironic style, particularly notable in the final passage quoted and in his use of the Latin phrase *inter vivos*!) In the first place it assumes that the classical curriculum was justified in Tudor and Stuart times. But it is not obvious that it was, nor, if it was, is it obvious that it was justified because the ethos of the period was a Christian neo-classicism. Certainly the ethos of the times goes a long way towards explaining why such a curriculum was adopted and generally approved of, but that is not the same thing as justifying it. Indeed, as Nidditch also points out, 'already in the seventeenth century the limitations of the contemporary grammar school curriculum (and practices) began to be emphasised'.[16] In other words it was felt precisely that the fact that it was a Christian neo-classicist age did *not* justify such a curriculum, which paid scant attention to such things as mathematics and science.

Secondly, even if it were argued that such a curriculum was justified at such a time, it does not necessarily follow that a science curriculum is justified in a scientific age. Argument by analogy is notoriously suspect, and rightly so, for it assumes that the two things that are being compared *are* analogous in important and relevant respects. To assume this generally involves begging a few crucial questions. And that is clearly the case here, for, whatever we say about the merits and demerits of a classical and a scientific curriculum respectively, it is clear that science and classics are not directly analogous.

This lack of comparability is well brought out by the suggestion that 'the doctrines and ethos of Christianity would be replaced by the teachings and implications of science and by humanly determined values for personal conduct and for relations *inter vivos*'.[17] For the determining of human values is in no sense a scientific task. It is true that an exclusive preoccupation with science may cause the individual to assume that religion, morality and even the aesthetic realm are mere superstition or catalogues of personal beliefs and attitudes which have no objective meaning or truth. But science cannot claim to have proved such a conclusion. An increased scientific understanding of the world may certainly lead to the need to reinterpret certain religious claims. For example, science has made it pretty clear that, if the claim that God exists is taken to mean that there is an anthropomorphic being who resides on one of the planets, then it is false. But science has not established that in no sense is there a God. Nor is it logically conceivable that it should.

Similarly, even if we understand 'science' in this context to include the human sciences as well as the natural sciences, science, though it may furnish data relevant to debate about moral values, can in no way finally determine what values we ought to adopt (or whether we ought to adopt any at all). There is an unbridgeable logical gap between determining what is the case and determining what ought to be the case – between description and prescription. Science is descriptive and not prescriptive.

The truth is that the classical curriculum, whether justified or not, differed from the proposed science curriculum in this important respect: such was its nature that it included a religious, moral and aesthetic dimension. Whether its treatment of these dimensions was in any way adequate, from our point of view, is another matter entirely. All I wish to stress here is that the classical curriculum of the past is not analogous to a proposed science curriculum for the present. Consequently, even if for the sake of argument we concede that the classical curriculum was sufficient and desirable in its time, we need not accept that a scientific curriculum would be sufficient and desirable for our own time.

But is there perhaps a case for a more or less exclusively science curriculum, which can be made without the suspect reference to the classics curriculum of the past? Surely not, for reasons that have already been given, at least implicitly. It is true that we live in the Age of Science, both in the sense that our way of life is pervasively dominated by scientific advances, and, probably, in the sense that science has had the effect of diminishing the appeal of traditional attitudes to such things as morality and religion for many people. But to assume that therefore schooling should be given over to a scientific curriculum would be quite indefensible.

It would be indefensible because such a proposal would be based on a confusion and would lead to an unacceptable state of affairs. The confusion on which the case for such a curriculum would be based would be that between the conclusions that may as a matter of fact have been drawn from the advances in science and the conclusions that may logically be drawn. Once again I refer to the fact that we cannot logically conclude anything about such questions as the existence of God, the beauty of art, or how we ought to conduct ourselves, from the study and findings of science. And that remains so, even though a scientific outlook may as a matter of fact have occasioned some people to give particular kinds of answer to such questions. The sciences, as such, introduce us to one form of knowledge, one interpretative attitude and one type of awareness only. A schooling given over to science would presumably be a schooling designed to produce scientists: it would involve no concern for aesthetic, religious and moral sentiment and no concern for the second form of knowledge, distinguished above,[18] which is necessary to attempting to resolve certain questions in those areas.

For some that consideration will be enough to condemn the idea of an exclusively scientific education. But suppose somebody were to accept the point and say 'So what?' What would be wrong with the sort of society that such an education might be expected to produce? The answer is simple: it is reasonable to suppose that a society characterised by such a single-minded outlook would be vastly impaired in respect of pleasure. It is not only that it would fail to contribute to the development in individuals of what have proved to be sources of great pleasure, but it would also contribute nothing towards the whole range of questions related to the problem of how men should conduct their lives. In so far as a purely scientific education fails to touch upon matters such as human nature, other sources of pleasure and interest, and how men ought to live, surely a society of beings educated in this manner will have less chance of maximising pleasure than it might.

So much, then, for the untenable view that the secondary school curriculum should be exclusively scientific. But there is still the question of what place, if any, science should have in the curriculum. A more moderate version of the Age of Science thesis runs as follows: since we do live in an age dominated by science, it is important that everybody should have some understanding of it. The initial problem here is how we are to interpret the phrase 'some understanding' of science. Following Yudkin,[19] I shall consider the notion of understanding science under three heads: having some scientific facts at one's fingertips, understanding the workings of scientific method, and understanding 'the relevance of science' or its place in society.

On the face of it the suggestion that everybody ought to have some scientific facts up his sleeve is just the sort of claim that a utilitarian would make. What could be more utilitarian than to argue that, in the sort of world in which we live, it is desirable that people should understand how to mend fuses, how a car engine works, and so on? Clearly such an argument is utilitarian in the loose sense with which we are not concerned. But is there a utilitarian case for imparting such information, in the specific sense of utilitarian with which we are concerned? I doubt it.

As Yudkin remarks, it is in fact difficult to imagine an 'ignorance more harmless'[20] than ignorance of such matters as how a television or a car engine works. Does it really matter that at the present time many thousands of people are ignorant of such things? Does it matter to them as individuals or to the community as a whole? I cannot see any reason to suppose that it does. So long as we maintain a supply of specialist technicians, who can mend our televisions and cars for us, it is difficult to see how such ignorance in specific individuals harms the community, harms the individuals concerned, diminishes the overall experience of pleasure, or affects the quality of life in a community in any way at all.

A slightly different argument would be that, in a democracy, widespread scientific know-how of a more exalted kind is necessary, in that many political and social decisions involve scientific knowledge. For example, questions such as whether it is worth searching for oil in a specific area, or whether a channel tunnel is a viable proposition, demand for their resolution a degree of scientific understanding. The problem here is surely that the level of scientific knowledge required to cope with such questions is way beyond the level that we could realistically hope to attain with children, especially if it is already conceded that science will at best form only a part of the curriculum. Moreover the information we impart to schoolchildren will in all probability be out of date by the time they come to face such issues in adult life. 'It is estimated, for example, that the quantity of scientific and technological knowledge, expressed in terms of hard facts, is doubling at the present time in less than ten years.'[21]

All in all the sort of scientific facts that we would be likely to impart to children do not seem to be particularly important.

What about understanding the workings of scientific method? By the scientific method, I take it, is meant the process of observation, hypothesis, empirical testing of predictions, and, if necessary, the subsequent recasting of the hypothesis. On what grounds might one argue for the desirability of all individuals having such understanding? I suggest that two sorts of argument might be produced, neither of which is ultimately persuasive. The first is to the effect that it is desirable that all individuals should be aware of what scientists are up to; the second is to the effect that understanding the workings of scientific method is an important part of intellectual development. I shall look at these two claims in turn.

Yudkin's main concern is that people should come to have some understanding of 'the *relevance* of science', and he expands this phrase by adding 'when is it appropriate to launch a scientific investigation; what kind of evidence should we seek in solving a particular problem; how can that evidence be weighed?'[22] What he would hope to achieve, by means of science courses that seek to stress 'the structure of experimental science itself' with special reference to the mysterious process whereby fruitful hypotheses come to be generated and hence scientific advances actually made, is a scientifically literate citizenry:

'A scientifically literate citizenry will be able to make informed choices in the many areas of public and private life into which science now enters. Scientifically literate men will appreciate the activity of the research scientist as a blend of creativity and vigorous intelligence. Science will no longer appear as a mysterious force, uniquely powerful and slightly sinister. Scientific literacy is necessary so that man may no longer be controlled by science, but may be restored to his position as controller.'[23]

Yudkin's concern is primarily to suggest *how* science should be taught, assuming that it functions as part of a general education. As far as that goes I do not wish to quarrel with his well argued thesis. But our concern is whether there is a case for saying that science *should* function as part of a compulsory curriculum. Is there a case for insisting on a scientifically literate citizenry? I cannot see that there is, mainly because I do not see any evidence to support Yudkin's premiss that a scientific illiterate lives in fear of science as something slightly sinister that is controlling man.

It must be admitted, however, that if it were empirically the case that scientific illiteracy led to fear and anxiety, that consideration would constitute a good reason for attempting to combat it, from a utilitarian point of view. As I say, I know of no evidence to support the empirical claim, and that is why I do not see a good reason to promote scientific literacy here. Fortunately, as will become clear below, the matter need not be left in the air until such time as the empirical issue is settled, since I shall argue that there is good reason to initiate children into science, with the consequence that, if it is true that familiarity with the methodology of science minimises a source of anxiety, such anxiety will be minimised. But this argument in itself does not appear to be sufficiently well founded to lead to the conclusion that all children ought to study science.

Nor is there any obvious reason to desire that people should appreciate the true nature of the activity of the research scientist, any more than there is to desire that people should appreciate the true nature of any human activity. A case could be made, on utilitarian grounds, for saying that ideally every individual should appreciate the true nature of all human activities: such appreciation would no doubt tend to minimise fear, scorn, suspicion and distrust of others, as well as to diminish the likelihood of painful errors of judgement arising out of ignorance. But such a consideration does not help us to determine which human activities it is most important for people to understand, and it is clear that it is impossible in practice to develop understanding and appreciation of all human activities. On the assumption that science is not a particularly strong source of fear and anxiety for non-scientists, there seems no more reason to demand that people should appreciate the true nature of the research scientist's activity than there is to demand that people should understand the true nature of the educationalist's activity. (Incidentally, however, it should be noted that an important part of what many contemporary scientists seem concerned to convey to the general public about the nature of their activity, may very easily be catered for elsewhere in this curriculum. I refer to a point that Yudkin stresses and which is succinctly expressed by Ritchie: 'school physics has underplayed the role of hypothesis and intuition.'[24] Examination of the true nature of scientific reasoning and of the status of the findings of inductive reasoning in science is essentially an epistemological question belonging to the sphere of philosophy.)[25]

As to the central contention – that a scientifically literate citizenry would be able to make informed choices, and know when to launch a scientific investigation and what kind of evidence to look for – this surely takes us back to the question of what it is realistic to hope to achieve. Such an ability might well be desirable on utilitarian terms, although not necessarily particularly so, if it were the sort of ability that would enable the citizenry to make informed decisions, so far as the scientific aspect went, on matters such as medical, nuclear power and energy research. But it is surely absurdly unrealistic to imagine that a scientific component in a curriculum could possibly hope to achieve such a degree of scientific understanding.

The argument most commonly put forward for the study of science is the claim that it constitutes an unsurpassable intellectual discipline. Yudkin, it will be noted, refers to the 'rigorous intelligence' of the research scientist. Nidditch, perhaps ironically, refers to the critical-mindedness which enables the scientist to tackle anything. There is a widespread assumption that the trained scientific mind is in some general sense a good mind. This kind of argument for science is well put by Nisbet, who refers to the grammar of science as one of its strong claims for a place in the curriculum.[26] The grammar of science is taken to include its observation of the facts, the attitude of objectivity, the intellectual honesty and the cautious drawing of conclusions. To this Nisbet adds, as points in its favour, the tendency of scientific study to develop such qualities as patience, an indifference to prestige, self-control and an 'unhesitating willingness to publish all . . . results for the benefit of all humanity'.[27]

That all of these are attributes of the good scientist cannot, I think, be denied. But they are also, without exception, the attributes of the good classicist, the good historian, the good geographer, the good social scientist, and so on. In order to justify teaching science, rather than certain other things, to all children on these kinds of ground, one would need to establish either that some of these characteristics could not be developed by any other study, or – a weaker case – that proficiency in science led automatically to proficiency in other spheres as a result of the development of these qualities. Neither claim is true.

Of course if an individual has learnt to be patient, indifferent to prestige, objective and intellectually honest in respect of science, there is a fair chance that he will be so in other spheres. One cannot guarantee that he will be, but he is at least more likely to be than one who has never developed patience and a concern for intellectual honesty in any other sphere. But then, by the same argument, we might dispense altogether with science and teach, say, history, on the grounds that it may develop such qualities just as well. In point of fact, however, neither study of science nor study of history could guarantee the active transference of such qualities to any other sphere, and proficiency in either one could not in itself lead to proficiency in the other.

The truth is that though science may serve as well as many other things to develop a critical and rigorous attitude, it does not breed any general competence – certainly not for matters that lie in the realm of the other form of knowledge, and probably not for other disciplines which though they are branches of the scientific form of knowledge are nonetheless distinct in a variety of ways.[28] All that is necessarily lost by not studying science is scientific know-how and ability, and the opportunity to display honesty, patience, concern for evidence, etc. in that sphere.

So what is the place of science in the curriculum? I will begin my conclusion to this section with a final reference to Nidditch.

'Science is the most effective, progressive and fruitful instrument available to man for discovering facts, regularities and grounded explanations, about the nature of things – about physical systems and about organic systems, including human mind and behaviour. And it is an instrument, with those qualities, for altering and controlling man himself and his environment for ends that he deems to be best. This power of alteration and control makes science man's vital hope and need in his attempts helpfully to resolve problems about the utilisation of human and material resources. Further, the freedom of thought, the broadening of view and comprehension, and the enlargement of the scope of action and opportunity have in the past been won primarily on an outcome of science and its diffusion, and science is man's most reliable assurance of their future continuation and growth. Science is the innocuous destroyer of superstition and prejudice, and of all that shuts mankind off from the knowledge it could achieve and of all that divides man from man. I shall mention one final reason that may be urged by proponents of the kind of scientistic thesis under consideration. It may be pointed out that the practice of science is widespread and the consequences of science are deep and extensive, nationally and internationally; it is improbable that any external forces can be applied to divert, still less to bring to rest, this massive movement. But it is undesirable to let the interests and activities of the scientists lie beyond the circumspection and critical evaluation of the non-scientists, who form the majority of the educated population. This circumspection and critical evaluation presuppose the necessity of an education that is chiefly in science.'[29]

Some of these claims are grossly inflated ('science is the destroyer of all that divides man from man'), and the whole paragraph is dangerously misleading in that it implies that there are virtually no significant questions that are not scientific in kind, and that scientific knowledge alone can in principle produce the Good Life and the Ideal State. Nonetheless, what I have tried to suggest in the previous pages is that substantially these claims are legitimate, so far as they go, and provided that we recognise that they are claims relating to the nature of science. If they furnish anything, they furnish an argument for the continued study of science. They do not constitute an argument to show that every individual ought to study science. The only obvious exception to that remark is the final point that non-scientists are in no position to keep an eye on the interests and activities of scientists. This is obviously true, but there does not appear to be any good reason to accept the idea that we are in danger of being exploited by mad or self-interested scientists.

Attempts, such as Ritchie's attempt to justify physics in the curriculum,[30] to justify the natural sciences by reference to the way in which they might be taught to meet something like Bloom's objectives, we reject on the grounds that such justification may be given for any other subject. Similarly Eggleston's helpful list of the seven major components that characterise the discipline biology indicates that the only components that are peculiar to the discipline are its specific concern (to study living organisms from a certain point of view) and some of its concepts.[31] To justify teaching biology rather than, say, history or physics, would require an argument relating to the value of its actual concerns for the individual student. 'When one considers the reasons why chemistry should be taught in schools', writes Coulson, 'two important considerations come to mind. The first of these is the need to attract some young men and women to a career in which chemistry plays a part. The second is the part that the subject can play in the totality of experience essential to educated citizens.'[32] In a sentence, my argument so far in relation to all the natural sciences amounts to saying that the first consideration is indeed important, but the second is untenable.

The only positive argument we have for the idea that it is valuable for each individual to study science is that, without any such study, the individual might in theory lack any awareness of the need for a certain kind of procedure in relation to a certain type of problem. This seems, at best, a weak argument for a minimal initiation into science.

But what is quite clear is that science is a complex business, a business that may afford great pleasure to the individual concerned with it, and a business of great value to the community as a whole, judged from the standpoint of pleasure. We want scientists, and ideally we want all people who would enjoy being scientists to be scientists; conversely we do not want to commit people to the study of science who do not find it suits them. The conclusion is obvious : all children should be initiated into science for a period of time that is sufficient to give them a clear idea of what studying science really involves. This will ensure, in so far as it is possible to ensure anything, that everybody is in a position to make a reasoned choice as to whether he wishes to pursue this important activity. It will also incidentally provide that basic understanding of science that some seem to feel is necessary to offset fears and inflated awe of the scientist. It may also be added that a basic grounding in science will prove to be of considerable value to those who subsequently take up certain trades, such as those of motor mechanic or television engineer.

Given the object of the exercise I conceive of this initiation being into something like general science or an integrated science course. Perhaps however physics and chemistry have the edge over biology in that the latter is to some extent derivative in practice on the former. It would be easier for one who was familiar with chemistry to find out about and make an informed choice as to whether he wanted to take up biology as an option in the tertiary stage than it would for a biologist to make an informed choice about chemistry. It has been argued that biology furnishes particularly useful facts. 'If I know that my wife's father was a haemophiliac, I may decide against having children because I also know that this is an inherited disease, sex-linked, which has a 50-50 chance of appearing in my sons.'[33] But such an argument is not very persuasive : there are occasions on which such biological facts would be very useful, but how common are the occasions?

I have dealt at some length with the question of the place of science in the curriculum for these reasons. (1) Science provides a good example of the sort of pursuit that many, misunderstanding the nature of a utilitarian approach to the curriculum, might wrongly assume to be a most important school subject on utilitarian terms. (2) In particular it provides a good opportunity to draw the distinction between the value that an activity may have in itself, on utilitarian terms, and its value or lack of it as an educational study. This point may be well summarised by reference to medicine: that the study of medicine is a worthwhile activity on utilitarian terms is beyond dispute. But it does not follow that it is worthwhile for all children to study medicine. (3) It illustrates a basic principle in the construction of the utilitarian curriculum: the curriculum should seek to provide the individual with the wherewithal to make genuinely informed choices for himself as to which activities he wishes to pursue. But this intention of making choice real is not based, as it is in the theories of White and Dearden, on the premiss that autonomy is a supreme value.[34] Rather it is based on the premiss that maximisation of pleasure is the supreme value. We cannot predict or pontificate on what activities are most pleasurable for particular individuals. But the more we can open up to individuals the possibility of informed choice between activities, the more chance have they of finding true satisfaction for themselves.

b. *Mathematics*

The argument here can be brief, since in many respects it is similar to the argument in relation to the natural sciences. By mathematics I mean the study of such things as algebra, geometry and trigonometry, and the normal claim made for this study would appear to be that it involves entering into a specific type of language or a 'vehicle for thought'[35] in relation to specific kinds of problems. This language, it will also often be said, is of great practical value, and, furthermore, to speak it well – to be a good mathematician – requires a high degree of 'concentration and application'.[36] 'Mathematical thinking constitutes one of the most fruitful, exacting and exciting modes of operation the human intellect is capable of', writes Nisbet.[37]

None of this, I think, is worth disputing. The language of mathematics is indispensable to the solution of many kinds of problem. Without it, indeed, most of the natural sciences could scarcely proceed: physics without the application of mathematics, for example, would certainly not be what it is today. If it is true to say that we need scientists, then it is no less true to say that we need competent mathematicians. And a competent mathematician certainly requires an exacting degree of concentration and application.

But, as in the case of the natural sciences, this only amounts to an argument in support of the claim that there should be mathematicians. Nothing so far indicates that it is desirable that any particular individual should engage in mathematics. Nor does it appear that there is any argument to support such a conclusion. If the suggestion that science constituted an awesome mystery, the terrors of which needed to be dissipated by understanding, was implausible, such a claim would be absurd in relation to mathematics. People do not walk in fear of a world dominated by algebra and trigonometry. There are no grounds for claiming that anyone would sleep more easily in his bed, if he had some inkling of the nature of geometry.

Again the fact that the good mathematician needs to have concentration and application, to which we may add other qualities such as precision and clear-mindedness, must not be confused with the claim that the study of mathematics leads to the development of these qualities, in such a way that they are automatically transferred and brought to bear on other different problems and aspects of life. The successful teaching of mathematics will lead to the development of such qualities in respect of mathematics, by definition, and no doubt an individual who has developed such qualities in this sphere is more likely to show concentration and application in other spheres than an individual who has not developed these qualities in any sphere. But the fact remains that the critical and analytic mathematician will not necessarily exhibit the same concentration and acumen in respect of, say, a moral problem. And even if, as a matter of fact, he is *disposed* to consider the moral problem in an exacting manner, as a result of the exacting attitude to mathematics that has been cultivated, he will not be *able* to do so without some experience of the moral sphere. In short all that the study of mathematics necessarily leads to is the development of a competent and critical mind in respect of mathematics. To this may be added the possibility that such an attitude will inform his thinking in other spheres; but of course the attitude alone is not enough, and the attitude as such might be acquired in many other areas of study.

But, it may be suggested, mathematical knowledge in the sense of the ability to understand and use geometry has an immediate utility or practical value for the individual. This is surely true; the question really is how great is its practical value, and is it of sufficient value to warrant a certain amount of educational time?

It should be remembered that the practical value of numeracy and the ability to calculate is not here in question. That the individual might nowadays suffer through being innumerate and unable to calculate is conceded, but our curriculum already contains provision against that contingency. Would the individual, *does* the individual, who lacks the kind of competence in the spheres of algebra, trigonometry and geometry that might normally be acquired in two or three years of study, suffer to any marked extent as a result? Would his ignorance cause any suffering to others, either directly or indirectly?

These are not the kinds of question that admit of any precise answer. But that does not mean that it is not entirely reasonable to assert roundly that the answer in each case is 'no'. The actual knowledge acquired from even the sixth form study of mathematics does not contribute much to the practical business of private life for the individual; it has little, if any, obvious bearing on the question of his own or anybody else's happiness, save in so far as the individual happens to take pleasure in the study itself.

Some, such as Alan Bishop,[38] have of course tried to argue otherwise. I can only say that I do not find any such arguments with which I am familiar convincing. Bishop, for instance, tries earnestly to argue from a real-life problem about what the best route to the airport is, by means of a claim to the effect that his mathematical ability helps him to construct the chapter he is writing, to the use of the mathematical method in relation to the problem of getting a man to the moon. The last example clearly shows the need for mathematical ability, but then most of us are not concerned with getting a man on the moon. The first example shows clearly that mathematical knowledge is *not* a great deal of help in such a problem. Whether it has helped Bishop to write his chapter I must leave others to judge for themselves. It is perhaps instructive to note that finally he falls back on the claim that 'mathematics more than any other subject relies on, and develops' the use of 'logical argument', as the main justification for teaching the subject.[39] Whether it is true that it necessarily relies on logical argument more than a number of other subjects might well be disputed. But the real answer to that claim is that one can develop a concern for logic without studying mathematics, and the ability to be logical in mathematics will not in itself help you to be logical about race-relations, what job to apply for, what party to vote for, or indeed anything except mathematical problems.

My conclusion is that there is no case for suggesting that all individuals ought to study mathematics, if we are thinking in terms of a necessary contribution to the pleasure of those who study it, or to other people as a result of their having studied it. On the other hand, mathematics, like the natural sciences of which in practical terms it is an indispensable part, is a complex discipline into which one needs careful guidance and initiation. That there should be mathematicians is of extreme importance, from a utilitarian point of view. Therefore, just as in the case of the natural sciences, we are forced to the conclusion that mathematics should constitute a compulsory two-year element in the curriculum.

Such provision provides all with the opportunity to grasp the nature of the activity, and hence contributes to their chances of realistically determining whether it is to their liking. The fact that mathematics forms a part of or contributes to many other activities, which the individual may subsequently choose to engage in, provides an additional reason for supporting its inclusion as a compulsory element. And finally, if I am wrong in my empirical claim that the study of mathematics does not have any real bearing on practical life and the pleasure to be derived therefrom, it may be added that some basic understanding of the nature, function and use of geometry, algebra and trigonometry is nonetheless provided. If that proves beneficial to the individual, well and good.

c. *Religion*

I have suggested that there are fundamentally two distinguishable ways of looking at the world or two interpretative attitudes: the scientific and the religious.[40] The distinction may be put crudely in this way: a religious attitude is based on some article of faith; a scientific attitude takes nothing on trust. There is no suggestion that a scientist cannot be religious. To be a scientist is not the same thing as having a scientific interpretative attitude. What is meant is that at rock bottom there is a conflict between interpretations of the world which are based on interpretative principles that are hypothesised, such as the Marxist, Christian or Buddhist interpretations of the world, and an interpretation of the world that will have no truck with any such religious interpretation.

You cannot, by definition, give people both interpretative attitudes, since they are mutually incompatible. But what you can do is indicate the existence of both, seek to explain the nature of either one, and, in promoting awareness of either standpoint enable people to decide for themselves which one they feel the need to adopt.

But what is the argument for so doing? It cannot be an argument based simply on an appeal to the value of truth, since the nature of these rival interpretative attitudes is such that, by definition, neither kind can be known to be true. Nor, I think, can one reasonably argue for introducing people to both kinds of interpretative attitude on grounds of autonomy or freedom alone, since there are some beliefs and attitudes at least that one would not think that people should be free to hold. That being so, one would need an argument to show that this particular freedom should be granted. If it is conceded, as I imagine it will be by most people, that, for instance, we see no compelling cause to introduce children to the doctrine of Nazism just so that they should be in a position to adopt it, if they choose to, then it follows that we cannot consistently base our argument for introducing them to Catholicism on the grounds that they should be in a position to adopt it, if they choose to, alone. We should need some argument that explained the difference between being free to adopt Catholicism and being free to adopt Nazism. Whatever that argument was, it would evidently have to go beyond an appeal couched only in terms of freedom.

The argument for introducing people to both kinds of interpretative attitude is surely that, in a variety of ways, such a procedure is likely to minimise pain and increase pleasure in the world. Awareness of both types of attitude and appreciation of the fact that neither one represents an indisputable truth denied only by foreigners, fools and fanatics, is necessary to understanding people who are different and being tolerant towards them, necessary to a personal commitment to an ideology that is non-dogmatic, and necessary to making an informed decision for one-self in a matter which may have significant repercussions for one's personal comfort.

Once again, I surely do not need to carry out an empirical demon-stration to convince the reader that a blind and single-minded devotion to any one specific interpretative attitude is likely to go on being, as it has historically been, a most potent source of pain in the world. I am not thinking only of the fact that people fight wars on such issues. I am thinking also of the more pervasive but equally damaging lack of respect, tolerance and understanding that often accompanies the ignorant assumption that one's own interpretative attitude represents not simply a belief to which one is committed, but a known truth to which anybody worth taking seriously *must* be committed. I would not claim either that awareness and understanding of the two different types of interpretative attitudes, and of different specific examples of the religious attitude, necessarily leads to sympathetic understanding and tolerance nor that such tolerance necessarily cannot come about with-out it. But it nonetheless seems a matter of common sense to suppose that awareness and understanding of rival attitudes is likely to contribute to such tolerance.

I must confess that I have argued elsewhere for the legitimacy of attempting to promote complete commitment to a specific ideology within a society.[41] But that argument was in the context of an ideal situation. In the world as we know it, in which there are many people committed to each of the two distinct interpretative attitudes (and many subdivisions within the religious interpretative attitude), and in which many derive considerable comfort from either one, it is surely impera-tive that there should be appreciation of both. Thus may we hope for an individual commitment that is based upon a genuine assessment of what the alternatives offer to the individual, rather than on the pressures and influence of the community, and a decrease in fanaticism and intoler-ance.

In curriculum terms such considerations necessitate an active intro-duction to the religious interpretative attitude through its various sub-divisions. Although doing science, history, etc. is not to be identified with having a scientific interpretative attitude, one may reasonably surmise that a curriculum predominantly geared to the pursuit of empirical knowledge would, in the absence of positive counterbalance, lead to the unthinking adoption of a scientific interpretative attitude. The school should therefore provide positive counterbalance by the study of the religious interpretative attitude. Given the nature of the argument for providing it, one would hope for an informative introduction to various religions covering a wide spectrum. There would clearly be practical problems in trying to do too much, but one might hope at least for some study related to Christianity, Buddhism and Marxism.[42]

As to the actual components of such a course I can hardly do better than quote extensively from Howard Marratt (though the reader should bear in mind that Marratt confines the term religion to a more traditional conception that I do).

'First factual knowledge and information: this will include events, practices (both ritual and moral), beliefs (both religious and moral) and writings (including myth), since too much religious and anti-religious fervour springs from ignorance of these facts; second, a study of religious communities in order to understand the interpretation given to the "facts" of the religion, for the first components can only be properly understood existentially in relation to the community . . . which is committed to a religious interpretation; third . . . will be a sympathetic insight into the nature of religious experience, an understanding that will involve both reason and emotion of why people feel and think about things in a religious way, of what is involved in religious experience . . . The object is not conversion or indoctrination but a careful understanding of and empathy with the religion.'[43]

To this I would only wish to add the importance of locating and drawing attention to the fundamental and key hypotheses within each religion, in order that at a later stage (see below) the status of these fundamental axioms may be examined.

d. *Fine arts*
One of the problems that beset many fine arts courses, particularly in colleges of art, is the relative weight to be attached to something that may loosely be described as aesthetic response and expression on the one hand and the history of art on the other.[44] This is not a problem that need worry the school, for the art college and the school have different functions. The former exists to produce artists (teachers of art in many cases, but nonetheless practising artists), and one may therefore reasonably argue about whether the study of the history of art is or is not necessary or conducive to the development of the true artist. But the school does not exist to produce artists, nor is there any obvious reason to accept that it should. The art teacher in schools 'is concerned to help

ordinary boys and girls to think and feel artistically, to understand art as an element in the growth of human beings, to see art in its historic and social contexts, and to grasp in what ways art might continue to be meaningful to themselves'.[45] In introducing the fine arts, then, I am not thinking in terms of attempting to produce creative artists.

What I mean by a fine arts course in the school context is a course designed to introduce children to music, painting and architecture and to help them to develop some understanding of these art forms. What do I mean by 'understanding' here? I do not mean coming to see the point or significance of such things in some metaphysical sense. I do not mean coming to appreciate, in the sense of respond sympathetically to such things. Either of those types of understanding might well follow from the sort of course I envisage, but what I mean by developing understanding of works of art is something rather more basic. I mean helping the child to recognise features of various works, helping him to 'understand' in the everyday sense of seeing what is going on or what is involved in a particular work of art.

Thus I envisage talk about harmony, leitmotifs, chords, atonality and so on in music, about light and shade, pattern and surface in painting, about style, workmanship and construction in architecture. This might be referred to as instruction in the vocabulary of the fine arts, the object of the exercise being to introduce works to the child, many of which he might not otherwise meet, and to explain them to him in such a way as to contribute to the development of a critical competence in the spheres in question.

What is the case for taking up valuable time with this exercise? It falls into two parts, as follows. The aesthetic, I have suggested, is one fundamental type of awareness. Furthermore aesthetic awareness or sensibility is indubitably a potential source of great pleasure. So, of course, are numerous other things, ranging from bingo to doing biology, for a great many people. But aesthetic pleasure differs in important respects from the pleasure to be derived from bingo or biology. First the fine arts are all-pervasive in a way that bingo and biology are not. That is to say architecture and music, and to a lesser extent painting, surround us. The opportunity to indulge the tendency to see beauty is ever present. Conversely the fine arts, particularly architecture, are intrusive on our lives in such a way that those who do have some aesthetic awareness may be actively displeased by a world in which local councils or property developers proceed without an inkling of an aesthetic dimension to experience. Thirdly, except in occasional instances, it seems indisputable that aesthetic appreciation is a far more complex matter than enjoying bingo, and far harder to explain to or cultivate in people. We may summarise this crudely by saying that the fine arts are a potent source of pleasure or displeasure, depending on how they are handled and where they inevitably touch on people's lives, for both producer and consumer, but that understanding of the fine arts is a complex and sophisticated business. This adds up to a strong case for devoting school time to initiating children into the aesthetic dimension.

But there is a second question that needs to be resolved and that is whether the kind of course I envisage would meet the ideal of contributing to aesthetic sensibility. Presumably there is no reason to suppose that it necessarily would, nor, conversely to suppose that, without such a course, individuals could not have developed aesthetic awareness. However such an admission need not lead us to deny that it is reasonable to suppose that in most cases aesthetic sensibility can be cultivated and will not arise spontaneously. The introduction of children to works with which they would otherwise in all probability remain unfamiliar, and the attempt to explain those works and cultivate a critical response to them, cannot but tend to train aesthetic sensibility.

One further question is what kind of works are envisaged. It should be clear that I am not proposing a course designed to enforce enthusiasm for a fixed heritage of good works. I am seeking to provide the opportunity for all people to find pleasure in the aesthetic, and to decide for themselves whether pleasure can be taken by them in the contemplation of the fine arts. Whether they decide affirmatively, and, if they do, whether their view of what works are admirable will coincide with yours or mine, are questions the answers to which I am not trying to legislate for. Consequently it would be a mistake to think that such a course must concentrate exclusively on the generally accredited masterpieces of the art world.

However, the contrary view that anything will do must be challenged. Pop music and pop art, for instance, may well have their place in the sort of course I envisage, since they may be used as vehicles for introducing the vocabulary of the fine arts. But such examples must not be concentrated on exclusively. This is partly because such exclusive preoccupation would conflict with the objective of introducing and explaining to the child those works of art which, in the normal course of events, would probably remain alien to him, and partly because much 'pop' material is not very complex. It is not that complexity is a virtue in itself, but if the child is not introduced to complex works and helped to understand them, he is not being put into a position in which he could derive aesthetic satisfaction from a great deal of art. For a great deal of art is just complex. Pop music may or may not be a valid art form, whatever that means, and it may or may not be as good as other music in some sense. But, with certain specific exceptions perhaps, it is musically considerably less complex than classical music. One thing is certain: without understanding of the latter, one cannot be in a position to judge the rival merits of the two.

I am therefore proposing a compulsory two-year initiation into the vocabulary of the fine arts. Such provision, as in the case of science, allows us to hope that some will come to feel that a life devoted to the fine arts is the most satisfactory life for them. Thus the community ensures the continued existence of artists, which we know from experience to be an indirect source of pleasure to many. Others, presumably the vast majority, will not choose either to practise as artists or to continue the study of the fine arts. Of these some will have acquired a basic ability to understand and thereby gain pleasure from the arts. For some it will in effect turn out to have been time wasted. But at least we shall have done our realistic best to open this source of pleasure to all, many of whom would not have found it without our help.

It is worth summarising this section in such a way as to indicate clearly the general principles whereby I am distinguishing between activities with reference to pleasure, while acknowledging that in most cases one cannot lay down hard and fast rules about which activities necessarily provide most pleasure.

Since a man may, for all I know to the contrary, experience as much or more pleasure from watching football as from listening to music, and since neither of these examples obviously involves an indirect contribution to the pleasure of the community as a whole in the way that the pursuit of science does, why is the latter made part of the compulsory curriculum and the former not? The answer is simple, but nonetheless important for that : it is more *difficult* to gain pleasure from listening to music. It is more difficult in two senses. First there is a pleasure that is dependent on understanding music, and understanding music is more complicated than understanding football. (There is also, it seems certain, pleasure that can be experienced in listening to music by those who do not understand music. I am not primarily talking about that pleasure, but even here the musical and the football case differs significantly in that for most children pressures or opportunities to watch football are likely to exist to a considerably greater extent than pressures or opportunities to listen to music, without the active participation of the school.) Secondly it seems tolerably clear as a matter of empirical fact that taking pleasure in music comes less easily to most people in the normal course of events than taking pleasure in sport.

I am not suggesting that listening to music is necessarily more worthwhile. I am not suggesting that the pleasure it provides is necessarily greater. I am not suggesting that its complexity or the difficulty associated with it, is a point in its favour. I say only that when we are considering the relative claims to curriculum time of two activities, whose contribution to pleasure is confined to the pleasure of the individual agent's experience, then difficulty or complexity is a relevant criterion. Although I do not accept White's distinction between two categories of activity, I have indicated that I accept what seems to lie behind his attempt to formulate such categories: [46] namely the observation that some activities are easier to understand than others, and that understanding is a necessary condition of taking pleasure in an activity. Pleasure must necessarily be increased in a community, if all individuals are in a position to know from experience what of all available options they most enjoy doing. That ideal cannot realistically be achieved. But what we can do, through the school, is seek to provide the understanding which is necessary to pleasurable participation in activities which we see reason to regard both as potentially highly pleasurable and as difficult to appreciate without initial guidance. We have no more grounds for supposing that everybody would be happier if we allowed them to grow up taking pleasure in readily accessible activities such as sport, and did nothing to help them find pleasure in the fine arts, than we have for supposing the contrary. That being so, in the interests of maximising pleasure, we ought to keep our options open. A greater effort is therefore required on behalf of the more difficult and complex.

If it be asked why we do not in that case introduce children to the extremely complex, but potentially pleasurable, activity of studying Greek as a compulsory element in the curriculum, the answer will once again be a commonsense one: because Greek is likely to be too difficult for some children, and we have much less reason to suppose that the ability to read Greek is likely to be a source of pleasure to them than we have to suppose that the fine arts will be.

Finally it should be added that the mere fact of seeking to extend understanding of the fine arts to all children is likely to contribute to diminishing pain to no small extent, inasmuch as it tends to combat feelings of hostility and resentment arising out of a sense of cultural differences. The fine arts will continue to exist and provide a source of great pleasure to some, whatever the schools do. But if the schools do nothing, there is a real possibility that interest in the fine arts will remain predominantly the interest of a certain social class. This in turn may lead to the sort of confusion exhibited by Murdoch (see above) whereby a contingent fact is interpreted as a necessary truth; the fact that the fine arts are by and large the interest of a particular social group is interpreted as indicating that that is their sole *raison d'être* and that there is no good reason to value them. Once appreciation of the fine arts is viewed as a feature of a particular social class and nothing more, the way is open for lack of sympathy and understanding either way.

The utilitarian is most concerned that differences between people shall be the outcome of their choice, so far as is possible, and not the outcome of limited opportunities, for only thus can we minimise resentment, fear and envy, which feelings are repugnant to utilitarianism.

e. *History*

The argument so far has been that in a community such as ours, given what we know of the range of human interests and pleasures at the present time, there is a strong utilitarian case for the existence of scientists, mathematicians and artists. In addition there is a strong case for introducing all people to an awareness of the religious interpretative attitude and the domain of aesthetic awareness, even if these turn out to mean little to them individually. But all four of these subjects, to use a neutral term, are complex. The average individual will need to be initiated into them before he can meaningfully determine for himself whether he wishes to pursue them further. Since the pleasure of the community is increased if individuals choose to do things that really satisfy them, there is a need to put children in a position to make an informed choice. That is why these four elements are made compulsory in the curriculum. You have to get into the water, if you want to swim.

I turn now to history, which, with literature, differs from the previous elements in the suggestion that these are subjects which should be pursued for a greater length of time and in greater depth. The basis for this suggestion lies in the claim that the study of literature and history is worthwhile in a different way to the study or pursuit of science. The value of science lies in the indirect contribution that its findings make towards people's pleasure. It is worthwhile as an element in the curriculum because it is a means to producing competent and satisfied scientists. But the value of studying history and literature (leaving aside, as always, the pleasure that an individual may take in the study) lies in what the study may do for the individual, rather than in any findings of such study. In a nutshell, I shall argue that the *study* of history and literature contribute to maximising pleasure, whereas it is the *findings* of science that make science's contribution.

'Here and there . . . there are a few professional historians who still believe that history should be more than a professional or educational activity and should reach out to inform, instruct, enliven, and ennoble and render more profound the common heritage of man.'[47] That at any rate is the view of J. H. Plumb, who goes on to argue that the social purpose of the historian 'should be to explain to humanity the nature of its experiences from the beginning of time'. To this he adds his own particular explanation in terms of the idea of progress. His claim is that history demonstrates a pattern of progress that has led to 'an increase in civility'.[48] To the obvious challenge that some remarkably unpleasant and uncivil things have happened late in man's history, such as Hitler's dominance, Stalin's persecutions and Hiroshima, Plumb replies : 'These things are horrible: they ought to be stopped. But they can only be stopped if humanity expands the bounds of its progress and applies its rational powers to a greater area of its activity. That is, that it learns its lessons of history.'[49]

Here then we have a particular example of the view that the importance of history lies in what it has to teach us about the past. It is a variant of Voltaire's more general claim that we can draw lessons from the past, coupled perhaps with something of Leibniz's view that the value of history lies in its discovering 'the origin of things present which are to be found in things past; for a reality is never better understood than through its causes'.

If we ignore two other claims that may reasonably be made for the study of history, cited by J. L. Heydon in his perceptive review of the nature of historical study,[50] namely that it can be fun and that it can provide a refuge from the present, the only serious challenge to the 'lesson of history' thesis, comes from the view that history is to be valued primarily as an intellectual discipline.

Thus it may be claimed, as Heydon observes, that the procedures of historical study 'have vigorous and imaginative qualities of great value in dealing with human thought and human life in general'.[51] Or, as Nisbet puts it, the intellectual effort called for by such a subject as history consists of 'the massive organisation of an enormous variety of apparently heterogeneous elements and [requires] the mental acumen and perspicacity which discerns that the elements are not so heterogeneous after all'.[52] To this he adds the important suggestion that one advantage of history over certain other intellectual pursuits, from the point of view of the school curriculum, is that it can be studied to some advantage at very different levels of attainment.

The argument for history as an intellectual discipline will not do, I suggest, any more than the similar argument for the study of science. It is not that one would wish to dispute that a good historian needs and, by definition, will have such intellectual qualities. It is rather that appeal to the concern for precision, respect for evidence, imaginative deduction or hypothesising and so on, which may reasonably be regarded as hallmarks of the good historian, do not serve to justify the study of history rather than the study of science, classics and heaven knows how many other things which also demand the same intellectual qualities. Nor can we accept the argument that in that case it does not matter which of a number of subjects children study, for there is no evidence that a good historian will be a good scientist – the very obvious reason being that although similar general intellectual qualities are involved, science is distinct from history.

Why, then, do I suggest a continuous in-depth study of history for all students? The length of time proposed (five years) is to be explained simply by the nature of the task: what is required is proper historical enquiry, research and understanding and not merely the passive reception of facts. But clearly one cannot begin enquiry or research into a period without some kind of framework of events, dates, facts, etc. That framework may ultimately be severely modified or even rejected as a result of further research, but something in the way of a framework must be there to start from. I therefore envisage a programme that falls into two parts: the first, lasting through the secondary stage of the curriculum, is mainly concerned with imparting information, providing a framework, and developing enthusiasm and interest in the story of the past. The second, lasting through the tertiary stage, is concerned with developing historians, by which I mean developing a concern and ability to interpret, understand and explain the past and its relation to the present. But why put forward this objective?

My argument is a version of the Voltaire/Leibniz/Plumb model. But it lacks Voltaire's rather simplistic view of the way in which history repeats itself, and Plumb's idiosyncratic quasi-historicist interpretation of history. It must of course be open for the individual student to arrive at an historicist interpretation of history, if he feels there are good grounds for such an interpretation. But to teach history through, say, Hegelian or Marxist spectacles is not at all what I propose. Such an approach, which interprets events in the light of a preconceived principle of causality, is a denial of the essence of history as an intellectual discipline. And although the argument for teaching history does not primarily reside in the fact that it is an intellectual discipline, it nonetheless is one, and my argument for teaching it would be nullified if it were not treated as such.

Basically my argument for giving prominence to history in the curriculum is that the study of history may contribute to widening our horizons and sympathies in respect of the fundamental question of how men ought to live, in a way that science, the fine arts and even religion cannot. The study of history may provide us with a vivid realisation of different possible ways of life, different ideas, different ideals and different beliefs, values and attitudes. It may promote an awareness of how these differences may affect events, both consciously and unconsciously. It may bring home to us the extent to which man is indubitably master of his own fate to a significant degree (such a claim being in no way necessarily in conflict with any specific religious interpretative attitude). It may contribute to our understanding of the present and diminish our hostility to things that happen to be alien to our way of life, by making them familiar to us and explicable. More than this – it may teach the general lesson that what is unfamiliar and strange is not for that reason to be distrusted or despised.

These claims are not extravagant. I do not say that the study of history necessarily has these results. I say that the nature of the study is such that it may have these results, whereas the nature of science and a host of other activities is such that they have no bearing on such considerations. A study of fifth century BC Greece, to take but one example, would necessarily bring the student face to face with such diverse matters as problems of democratic government, slavery, homosexuality, the morality of Empire, totalitarianism, the effect of climate on national characteristics and way of life, and the function of drama or culture in general. We cannot predict with any certainty what the result of study of such matters will be in every individual case, but we can reasonably say that it is likely to lead to a wider perspective, greater understanding and broader sympathy. For it must be remembered that we are not here making claims about a university degree course, but suggesting that it is likely that schoolchildren would gain something from the study of history: the comparison has to be between the individual who is historically ignorant and the individual who is not.

But why is such widened awareness to be valued? On the grounds that it must tend to diminish insularity, fear, hostility, narrow-minded dogmatism and apathy. If a man lacked all historical awareness or perspective he might have some excuse for fearing and distrusting whatever he is unfamiliar with, for assuming that things are as things must be, and even for concluding that all is for the best in the best of all possible worlds. But for anyone with a fair degree of historical understanding such provincialism would be inexcusable. That the diminution of such provincialism is desirable on utilitarian grounds is obvious. To understand all may not quite be to forgive all, but to appreciate the accidental nature of so much that we might otherwise take to be necessary and right, and to have our minds opened to alternatives and made familiar with the mysterious and alien, must contribute something to tolerance and sympathetic understanding.

The argument for including science in the curriculum was that it would enable those who might derive pleasure from being scientists to appreciate the fact, it being clearly worthwhile that there should be scientists in the community. That being the nature of the argument, it follows that what is required is an initiation into science for all. The argument for history is now seen to be of a quite different order: its value lies not in the conclusions or findings that historians present to mankind, but in what the study itself gives to the individual. It may not give him any direct pleasure, but it is likely to affect his outlook and attitudes in a way that will lead to an increase in pleasure over pain in the community as a whole. On utilitarian terms it is worthwhile that there should be willing scientists, mathematicians and artists, but it is worthwhile that each individual should have the kind of perspective that, though it can never be guaranteed, can only be developed by a study such as history.

It may be added that since history is not introduced into the curriculum simply as a means to enable individuals to see whether they wish to pursue it, and is therefore envisaged as a study in some depth that will continue into the tertiary stage, it will serve well as a vehicle for developing general intellectual competence. I have already made it clear that I see no reason to accept some mysterious faculty that allows of competence in any sphere. But there are attitudes and skills which are common to many spheres. Perseverance, respect for evidence, imagination, etc. may all be developed through the study of history. This alone will not enable the individual to display such qualities in spheres he knows nothing about. But it may be hoped that it will lead him to exercise and respect them in everyday life and discussion. Once again this cannot be guaranteed, but at least the individual is in a position to display such qualities. The value of such qualities resides in their utility. A community in which people try to be reasonable, to argue with reference to the evidence, to persevere with complex problems and so on, will presumably be the happier for it.

Martin Booth puts it too strongly, too vaguely and too narrowly, I think, when he claims that it 'can be said with *certainty* . . . that a study of history – any history – brings about a freedom of mental movement and a heightened awareness of the present through its contrast with the past which enables him to stand more confidently in his own age'.[53] Nonetheless this kind of argument, I have claimed, is appropriate to the study of history in a way that it is not appropriate to the study of science, and is sufficient to justify the inclusion of history in the curriculum as a compulsory study. Given the object of the exercise, which is *not* to produce highly competent practising historians, although the manner of teaching in the tertiary stage must be such as to allow and encourage pupils to proceed as historians, world history rather than English history is demanded. The idea, in a phrase, is to let the unfettered mind play upon the myriad patterns of history – imaginatively free, but intellectually bound by concern for sound argument. What know they of England, who only England know?

f. *Literature*
On the face of it literature is the sort of discipline that does not seem

readily to find a utilitarian justification. As Hough puts it, the crisis facing literature is precisely that it lacks any obvious utility.[54] It does not pay, because it is not supposed to. Rather, it has always been claimed that its contribution is to enhance the quality of life. And reference to the quality of life is taken to be in conflict with the essence of a utilitarian viewpoint.

My claim is that just as science in schools is only immediately justified by considerations of utility in the crude sense of utilitarian, so valuing the study of literature is incompatible only with the crude sense of utility. Certainly studying literature does not fit one automatically for some essential social role, but, I shall argue, the study of literature is strongly to be approved on utilitarian terms in my more sophisticated sense of that word. I shall argue that there is good reason to assume that the widespread study of literature will contribute more to pleasure than the widespread study of, say, biology and hence certainly improve the quality of life, if we judge the quality of life by reference to satisfaction.

I should like to follow Hough further, since his criticisms of actual literature courses have some bearing on what I mean by the study of literature. He argues against a tradition concerned with 'the technique of "practical criticism" ' (meaning the close examination of small samples of verse and prose) and with the notion that 'the object of an education in literature must be to produce literary critics or scholars'.[55] The objections to such a 'literary criticism' approach are essentially three. (1) It is by no means obvious that there is any particular value in the close scrutiny of individual texts, beyond the pleasure such activity may give the individual agent. (2) There seems to be no evidence to support the contention that such competence leads to a general ability 'to distinguish the authentic from the meretricious in non-literary fields'.[56] (3) For the vast majority of students the goal of such a course is never reached. They do not approach the specialised competence of the literary scholar.

Hough's alternative view is that courses in the study of literature should seek to maintain their exemplary and ideal-forming role, affecting the character and attitudes of those who experience them, developing their sensibilities and perceptions. 'We expect a literary education to expand their range of human awareness and sympathy; to enlarge their imagination beyond the limits of their own class and country; to show them that our problems and obsessions are part of a larger pattern of human experience, and assume a new meaning within the larger pattern.'[57]

This is the kind of objective that I too have in mind, one that takes the emphasis off the detailed and minute examination of precise textual points (although some degree of precise attention will ultimately be needed), and puts it instead on the content and the intention that the content will be something vital and alive for the student. To this I would add the subsidiary, but no less important, objective of what Reuben Bower has called the cultivation of 'active amusement' in reading.[58]

The aim therefore is to help children to read with facility and pleasure, and thereby to expand their horizons and sympathies. The study of literature is thus seen as complementary to the study of history. Quite apart from the question of justification, this raises the question of whether and how such an objective may be achieved.

It is customary in some quarters to mock the pretentious claims of literature. And it is easy to do so, since they are not the kind of claims that are easily susceptible of proof. But it must be stressed that the difficulty of proving them does not establish their falsity, and they may yet be reasonable contentions. And certain points do seem clear : first, although Utopians such as William Morris may choose to imagine that in a perfect community children just would take up reading by the age of four,[59] people do not, as things are, take up reading of their own accord. They need careful initiation into it. Secondly, and conversely, there is abundant evidence that many people are put off reading by being plunged too early without sufficient guidance into material that is too complex for them and alien to their own outlook.

Thirdly, literature may serve as a necessary complement to history in promoting understanding of other ways of life and alien attitudes. There is surely some truth in Leavis's claim that 'if we want to go further than the mere constation that a century and a half ago the family counted for more than it does now, if we want some notion of the difference involved in day to day living – in the sense of life and its dimensions and in its emotional and moral accenting – for the ordinary cultivated person, we may profitably start trying to form it from the novels of Jane Austen'.[60] And fourthly there is need for the study of form as well as content, because appreciation of content is to some extent dependent on appreciation of form. As Leavis goes on to point out, 'only if we are capable of appreciating shade, tone, implication and essential structure' in Jane Austen can we profitably use her novels for the purpose of shedding light on the past, or, indeed, enjoy them.

So what is being proposed is a course in literature that realistically starts from material that is contemporary and familiar in content to the child, but which gradually expands outwards to the unfamiliar and foreign, attempting to sustain interest and develop awareness of the form throughout. Such a programme might well include some emphasis on the creative writing of the child in the early stages, taking creative to indicate nothing more startling than his own positive attempt to express himself via the written word. The argument for this would simply be that an attempt by the individual to find an effective form for his content would no doubt be salutary in developing an understanding of the interrelationship of form and content. The material for such a course does not have to be confined to the accredited great works of literature, but the objectives proposed will not be met if material is selected throughout on a basis of scorning every century but this and every country but our own. The proposed course is a course in literature, not a course in English literature. I therefore envisage the inclusion of material in translation.

The grounds on which I would advocate a full-scale literary element in the curriculum should by now be obvious. It has a certain value in that the ability to read well is contributory to facility of study in a number of other fields and to the ability to communicate generally in subtle and sophisticated terms. The likely contribution to pleasure is great, certainly for the individual who finds as a result of such a course that literature provides a potent source of satisfaction for him personally, but, more to the point, indirectly for the community as a whole. Literature is, as White says, a 'valuable instrument for enlarging one's acquaintance with ways of life and ideas'.[61] White, of course, is anxious for such wide acquaintance in order that each individual shall be in a position to make a meaningful choice as to which of these ways of life and ideas to adopt for himself. My point is that such acquaintance is contributory to the development of sympathy and understanding, even though it cannot in itself guarantee it. There is every reason to suppose that a world in which people had the perception, sympathies and awareness of a Tolstoy would be a happier place, even though Tolstoy himself was an irascible old gentleman at times.

The reason that this is likely to be so is simply that literature is about the human condition. Literature, from Simon Raven to Shakespeare, is 'predominantly concerned with human emotions and feelings'. It 'treats of people, their feelings, their relations with one another, their response to situations, the way in which they act, the reasons why they do so and the consequences of those actions. It introduces the reader to some of the complexities of people and their behaviour'.[62] The kind of awareness and perceptive understanding that literature presupposes is a necessary condition of a sympathetic and empathetic outlook. That kind of outlook is worth more, on utilitarian grounds, than a hundred useful knacks or social skills.

It should be added that this view of the nature and possible function of the study of literature should not be taken to imply some restricted conception of literature as a form of expression bound to realism, nor to imply anything about the nature or purpose of the writer. George Gissing wrote his early novels with this intention: 'I mean to bring home to people the ghastly condition (material, mental and moral) of our poor classes, to show the hideous injustice of our whole system of society, to give light upon the plan of altering it, and, above all, to preach an enthusiasm for just and high ideals in this age of unmitigated egotism and "shop".'[63] The bulk of his novels, however, were written in the light of a rather different creed : 'My attitude henceforth is that of the artist pure and simple. The world is for me a collection of phenomena, which are to be studied and reproduced artistically.'[64] But the change in Gissing's intentions, and indeed the change in the nature of his novels, makes no difference to the fact that all his novels contribute equally to providing something of the awareness and understanding of the human condition, to which I have referred.

The study of literature continues into the third stage of the curriculum for essentially the same reason as history : we are concerned with the value of studying literature for the individual, rather than with the value of there being some people who have studied literature. Time is needed for a thorough initiation into literature.

I referred above to 'a certain value' residing in the fact that the study of literature enhances 'the ability to communicate generally'. Although that is not my central claim for the justification of the study of literature, it will be appreciated that reference to it runs the risk of foundering in the controversy surrounding the apparently contradictory findings of Bernstein and Labov in respect of language codes.[65] I must stress, therefore, that I have not suggested that literature, being by and large the product of individuals who have what Bernstein terms an 'elaborated code', and hence being a written version of an elaborated linguistic code, is *ipso facto* more valuable than any product of a restricted code and should be used as a means of weaning those with restricted codes away to the adoption of an elaborated code. Nor have I defended literature primarily as a means to developing a 'flexible' language code, to use Bernstein's terminology, as a means to enabling the individual better to verbalise his intent, or increasing his ability to deal in context-free universalistic meanings.

As far as Bernstein's theory about language goes, I am in no position to comment either on the quality of his research or the accuracy of his specific findings, both of which have been criticised. Nor do I wish to enter upon arguments that centre upon the definition of 'working-class', a tedious term if ever there was one, especially now that we have been assured by Douglas Holly that 'the working class is really . . . nearly all of us' (that is everybody who is not 'a capitalist owner').[66] Nor do I want to argue with those who, following Labov, claim that research shows that working-class children, when given an opportunity to speak freely and at their ease, can be 'highly articulate', can have ideas and can express them, can avoid some unnecessary 'hemming and hawing, backing and filling'[67] which sometimes characterises a more educated speaker, and can use a language that is rich and expressive in its own right. (Honestly, one sometimes wonders what sociologists are up to. So much would seem to me to be a matter of common sense and personal experience.)

But I do wish to observe, without the benefit of organised empirical research, but without the disadvantage of conflicting empirical research, that it seems to me patently obvious that if you want to have a discussion that will accurately mirror the complexity, subtlety and minute distinctions that are part of the matter under discussion, about, say, the question of sovereignty and the EEC, you need more sophisticated linguistic skills than those apparently possessed by 'Larry' and others cited by Labovians in their attempts to refute Bernstein. If a discussion or the reasoning applied to a problem is to be subtle and precise then one needs a language that has the features of what Bernstein calls an elaborated code. Whether in general such language is more common in homes that may be defined as middle class, I neither know nor, in the present context, care.

The reason for this digression is this: throughout this chapter I am looking for what seem to me to be sufficient conditions for the inclusion of an element in the curriculum. That is to say, in respect of each element I am looking for a reason (or reasons) that, if it is present, is sufficient justification in itself. But this does not mean that other advantages may not stem from the inclusion of an element in the curriculum. As we have already seen, 'history' is not sufficiently justified by reference to its contribution to intellectual development, since many other studies, including the study of literature, could make the same contribution. But once we have a sufficient reason for including history, it is quite in order to add that it may make such a contribution, which carries the incidental consequence that we no longer need to worry about that particular objective.

In the same way, although I regard the function of literature as an eye-opener as sufficient justification for its inclusion in the curriculum, given the manifest utilitarian value of 'open eyes' in the sense in question, I should now like to add that its propensity to develop a relatively elaborated linguistic code is a further merit. It might not be of great value in a community that did not experience or want to experience any great degree of autonomy. But in a community where people have complicated matters to discuss, complicated choices to make and complicated decisions to reach, it is of value. Discussion and decision that is of any quality demands, amongst other things, precision and the ability to think in abstractions: most literature, even quite poor literature by conventional standards, is more precise and abstract than the day to day talking of most of us. For that reason too children are to be encouraged to read literature with understanding.

IV TERTIARY STAGE

a. *Vocational studies*

The tertiary stage of the curriculum involves the continued study of history and literature, the introduction of vocational studies and social studies, and the provision of a range of options. About the first two elements I need say no more. I will therefore turn now to vocational studies.

There has been a certain amount of talk in recent years about the significance for education of a likely increase in leisure time for adults in the future. The curriculum under consideration certainly caters for such an eventuality by its emphasis on such things as sport and literature, which though they may not be put forward primarily as sources of pleasure for the individual may obviously nonetheless prove to be pleasurable leisure activities, and through its programme of options (see below). But despite emphasis on the likelihood of increased leisure, most of us will still continue to have to spend an appreciable amount of time working.

Few educationalists, apart from Plato, have dared to say that pre-paration for jobs matters or that vocational training is an important part of the school's role. Where schooling has been vocationally oriented, it has been contemptuously dismissed as not being truly educational. No doubt one can go too far, as Plato perhaps did in making 'education' for some consist in no more than vocational training. But a utilitarian approach does lead to the conclusion that some concern to see that individuals find jobs that are suited to their talents and interests is a proper concern for somebody. A community will evidently be the happier for a wide degree of job satisfaction. And what agency is better suited to concern itself with this matter than the school?

What I envisage is a more serious and comprehensive attempt to do the job that in some schools is already done by a member of staff acting as careers adviser. Curriculum time should be devoted to opening children's eyes to the importance of thinking about what kind of employment they would like to find, to informing them of the sort of alternatives open to them with their particular talents and interests, and to giving them such mundane details as the skills necessary, the rates of pay, the type of promotion available and so on in respect of particular jobs. In addition, ideally, opportunities of gaining some experience of various jobs by visits should be provided.

It is, I suppose, to some extent because of the fact that the vocational element in the curriculum has historically been associated with less intellectually able pupils in secondary modern schools, that some find it hard to see concern for vocational studies 'as anything other than a twentieth-century version of Robert Lowe's belief that "the poor ought to be educated to discharge the duties cast upon them". Too great an emphasis on a vocational or directly society-orientated element in the curriculum cannot but reduce the autonomy of the pupil; nor is it with the passage of time a wise investment for our society because the shape and number of manpower cells are constantly changing.'[68]

My reply to this kind of argument is: I do not propose 'too great' an emphasis on the vocational element. The autonomy of the pupil is not necessarily the only important consideration, but in any case I see the provision of information about occupational skills together with experience of various occupations as a contribution to autonomy rather than antipathetic to it. It is precisely because 'the shape and number of manpower cells are constantly changing' that children need to be abreast of current trends and current opportunities, rather than left to find an occupation in the light of what they are familiar with as a result of their home and everyday life. Far from being a modern variant of teaching the poor 'to discharge the duties cast upon them', this is a proposal designed to bring it home to all pupils that no duties are cast upon them in respect of jobs.

This element is placed in the tertiary stage, because it presupposes some vaguely determined talents and interests in the individual. At the same time it is important that vocational studies should proceed *pari passu* with the options on the curriculum, since the intention to take up a particular job may necessitate taking on a particular option.

Of course such a scheme will not be entirely satisfactory. Many individuals will leave school still uncertain what to do, others will change their minds and discover that they are not qualified to do what they now want since they did not take up particular options at school, and some will still have no effective choice in what they do. But it is better that some attempt should be made to consider the future than that the matter should be ignored. It is worthwhile that the school should do what it can in terms of preparing the individual child to take on a job to which he is suited, because such preparation can only lead to an increase in personal pleasure for the individual. Greater personal satisfaction for individuals can only lead to greater harmony in society as a whole.[69]

b.   *Social studies*
Information – simple, blunt facts – has been one of the victims of the

overreaction against the traditional pattern of education. The criticism was launched that we mindlessly instilled irrelevant facts. The conclusion was drawn that facts did not matter. 'It is not what you teach', as the slogan has it, 'but how you teach that counts.' Clearly such over-simplification will not do at all. Nobody in his right mind could accept the implications of the slogan without qualification. How you teach thieving is neither here nor there. You should not teach it. Conversely, that a child should be taught to preserve his health is more important than the way in which he is taught this.

The utilitarian says that many facts are of considerable importance, since without access to them we are not in a position to estimate what should be done in various situations. And one sort of fact is particularly important – namely facts about the nature of society. Now at one level the question of what is going on in society – the social facts – is exceedingly complex, and the answer that one may give will be governed to a considerable extent by one's definitions and procedures in searching for an answer. But that is not the level of enquiry that I have in mind here.

All that I am proposing under the name of social studies is the imparting of some pretty basic information about how our democracy works, how the wealth is distributed, how many aged people there are, how many coloured immigrants, cultural differences between groups in the community and so on. Insofar as it is possible such information should be supplemented by familiarity with and experience of whatever is in question and, where relevant, by an attempt to explain the problematic nature of collecting evidence for answers in such a sphere. Thus one may explain how our democracy works in principle easily enough and supplement this by visits to local government meetings or whatever. But any attempt to pass on to the more subtle question of where power actually lies, should surely be supplemented by an attempt to indicate the shortcomings inherent in any attempt to make such an analysis (see section v, Philosophy).

Once again such social studies cannot guarantee a happier community. But it seems not unreasonable to suppose that the sort of awareness and knowledge envisaged would be likely to contribute to a more harmonious state of affairs. Goodness knows how many judgements are passed each day, how many opinions recorded, how many arguments disputed and how many decisions taken which are positively prejudicial to the welfare of some group or other, as a result of conviction that something which is in fact false is 'a well-known fact'.

c. *Options*

A complete list of options that might reasonably be made available to children in schools would be wearisome. I shall offer a selective list of examples, and then seek to outline some criteria for determining whether a particular option should be available or not. These are not options out of which the child must choose one or a certain number. If the individual child is not interested in availing himself of any of the opportunities afforded to him that is his affair: half the available time for schooling can be spent by him in some other way, as he chooses, away from school. This recommendation is a practical one and it is based on the assumption, which once again I take to be reasonable, that on balance more will be gained in terms of overall pleasure, if people are not forced to take on any of the options.

Such a proposal does not conflict with my argument for a compulsory basic minimum, provided that there is reason to suppose that the list of options does not contain any element that should be a compulsory element, according to the type of argument advanced for initiation into one or other of the compulsory elements.

All the elements of the curriculum into which the child has been initiated should continue as options on the curriculum. This goes without saying, given the nature of the argument put forward about the natural sciences, mathematics and the fine arts. We need scientists, mathematicians and artists to contribute to the general happiness. They are complex pursuits in which, except in rare instances, individuals cannot progress far without help and guidance. There is the additional point that many children may contemplate taking up trades or professions in which something more than an initiation into one or more of these elements would be an advantage, if not a necessary precondition. The same is not true of religion: we do not specifically need Christians, Marxists and so on, but clearly here is another complex field in which individuals may become engrossed and hence wish to study further, but in which they would benefit enormously from the guidance of those with expertise.

I offer the following as examples of options which should also ideally be available: geography, economics, psychology, sociology, Latin, French, cooking, carpentry, typing. And, as examples of pursuits that need not be options: photography, angling, dancing, mountaineering. Neither list is supposed to be exhaustive, and in fact I would not at this stage wish to appear too dogmatic or confirmed in my opinion of the contents of either list. Clearly any list of options would have to take some account of the local conditions: the availability of resources, the staffing, and the interests of the pupils. Thus a case might be made for something like mountaineering in a school set in the heart of a city, where certain members of staff have competence in the sphere, where children are interested in the idea, and where resources are available for doing it. But although I do not want to make too much of the lists, I shall seek to explain them as if they did constitute a reasonably firm selection of things to be offered and things not to be offered.

The criteria that I have had in mind in drawing up the two lists are three (over and above the question of pupil interest and available resources, including teacher expertise). (1) The complexity of a pursuit. (2) The usefulness to society in terms of contributing to its prosperous and harmonious maintenance. (3) The relevance to the individual. By this phrase I mean to draw a distinction between pursuits in which the individual is likely to have to engage anyway, at work or in the home, and pursuits which are likely to be hobbies or pastimes. The former I refer to as relevant pursuits.

Strong candidates for inclusion in the optional list are pursuits which meet all three criteria. An obvious example would be economics: it is the sort of study in which the average individual will benefit from the help of somebody with expertise in the field – it is complex enough to warrant guidance. It is useful to society to have economists and it will be relevant to the lives of those who intend to work in one of the many fields where economics plays a part. Much the same may be said of psychology and sociology, and, to a lesser extent, geography. I say to a lesser extent, because geography as such, as opposed perhaps to certain geographical information, does not appear to play a significant part in such a wide range of occupations as sociology. It is therefore likely to prove relevant, in my sense, to less people. One might also argue, although I shall not attempt to do so since it will not materially affect my curricular proposals, that geography is less useful to society than psychology.

This last observation does, of course, raise one of the two questions that need to be answered in relation to this first group of options. What exactly is meant by 'geography' here? For its value must to some extent depend on how we interpret the term. And, once it is clear what is meant, the second question to be asked is 'why are geography and the other options so far mentioned only options rather than compulsory elements in the curriculum?'

The study of geography can evidently involve a number of different pursuits. There are those geographers who, thinking of economic geography, population geography and historical geography, and eschewing the traditional emphasis on a specifically regional approach, conceive of their subject as something very wide indeed which may 'build one bridge over the abyss'[70] between the natural sciences and the study of humanity. Now clearly one might devise a specific geography course for schools which, though it centred on and stemmed from regional description and/or a real differentiation, was concerned to branch out into historical and sociological questions. Some programmes of environmental studies might fit this pattern. Would not such an approach, involving as it would some mathematics and some science, as well as introducing history and sociology to some extent, make geography an obvious candidate for inclusion in the compulsory part of the curriculum? There is no real answer to this in the abstract. It must depend upon the nature of the mathematical, scientific and historical aspects of the course. But what is clear is that we are now drifting over into the separate question of the organisation and methodology of the curriculum.

I have argued that all children ought to be initiated into the natural sciences and mathematics, and ought to study history in some depth. If those objectives can be met by some kind of integrated programme, I cannot see any good reason for objecting. Consequently, if a programme of studies can be devised that integrates or relates those disciplines through geography, there can be no cause for complaint. (I cannot see any good reason for saying that children ought not to be allowed to do geography!) My own feeling would be that a programme based on environmental studies, for example, would not be likely to convey a true understanding of mathematics and the natural sciences as such and could not possibly involve the sort of study of history that my argument demands. Therefore it would not be a satisfactory method in itself, and if it has to be supplemented by the separate study of mathematics, science and history, its contribution on those fronts becomes otiose. So although in principle geography might be defined in such a way as to make it an umbrella study that covered the elements (or many of the elements) that I have argued ought to be compulsory, it does not seem in practice that it is likely to be able to serve this purpose.

It is geography in the much narrower sense of 'the art of recognising and describing regions'[71] that I had in mind when placing geography amongst the options. It is geography understood as the attempt 'to describe and interpret the variable character from place to place of earth as the home of man'[72] that, I am claiming, cannot be justified as a compulsory element in the curriculum. Why not? Why are the geographer, the economist, the sociologist and the psychologist thus distinguished from the historian, the mathematician, the artist and even, heaven forfend, the Christian and the Marxist? A strange utilitarianism this, that concludes that Buddhism outranks economics in our day and age.

It must be remembered first that I am not trying to compare the worth of the sociologist and the Buddhist. I am not asserting that it is more worthwhile to study mathematics than to study psychology without qualification. I am arguing about what it is worthwhile for children to do at school. Now clearly none of the proposed options under consideration here are directly comparable to history and literature. One does not dispute that the geographer and the sociologist will have particular insights and look at certain situations from a distinctive perspective, as a result of their field of interest. Nonetheless history and literature stand alone in their potential for opening our eyes to the range of life styles, multitude of ideas, diversity of human nature and incalculable and awe-inspiring consequences of human actions. They have the capacity to broaden our understanding and sympathy, as no other pursuits do. Thereby they contribute to expanding our horizons and enabling us to face the fundamental question of how we ought to conduct our lives in an informed manner with a tolerant and open mind. Such consequences are worth more than any scientific discovery or psychological revelation on utilitarian terms.

But surely, it may be said, even if geography and economics are not comparable with literature and history, they are directly comparable with the natural sciences and mathematics. We need economists, geographers, psychologists and sociologists just as much as scientists and mathematicians, given the nature of our society, don't we? True. But the argument for initiating children into mathematics and the natural sciences was also based on their complexity. We need economists as much as mathematicians (I think that this is probably debatable, but let it pass); they are as valuable on utilitarian terms. But the suggestion is that as a result of the compulsory curriculum children will be in a position to appreciate the nature of economics, geography and so on once it is explained to them, and to undertake such pursuits, if they choose to; whereas I would argue that a child who had not studied mathematics or natural science *per se* would not readily understand what was involved in them. To explain what physics is to somebody who has no experience of the natural sciences at all would be extremely difficult. But to explain what economics is to someone who is familiar with science and mathematics, and is therefore familiar with an integral part of economics and with the methodology of the scientific form of knowledge, which is in principle common to such pursuits as economics, psychology and sociology, would be relatively easy.

Finally, it may be suggested that we could teach mathematics and science through or in relation to such things as economics and psychology. This is presumably true, at least in principle. But it is comparable to the attempt to argue for a wide conception of geography as a compulsory element in the curriculum, noted above. Provided that a genuine experience of mathematics and science is being provided by such a programme that is well enough as far as they are concerned. But on what grounds are we adding economics (or psychology or whatever) as a compulsory study for all children? The level of economic expertise that they will attain to will not contribute anything to their pleasure or anybody else's, either directly or indirectly. They do not need to study it in order to be in a position to understand what it is, so we do not need to provide experience of it in order to allow them to make an informed choice as to whether it is the sort of pursuit likely to interest them. There being no obvious grounds for making it compulsory, it remains an option, as do psychology, geography and sociology.

I turn now to French and other modern languages. They gain a place as options largely on the score of complexity. They are pursuits which many may wish to undertake and in respect of which a teacher may prove of no little benefit. (If there is truth in the empirical claim that personal tuition in this sphere is of no great value and that language laboratories can do the job well and quickly, I would argue for dropping modern languages from the curriculum altogether. The expense of equipping all schools with language laboratories to cope with an option, when they are available elsewhere already, hardly seems justified.) They also have limited social usefulness and relevance.

At a time when more and more children, at younger and younger ages, are being introduced to French, my suggestion that it should at best be reduced to the status of an option calls for some comment. First, I see no warrant whatsoever for the claim that ' the ability to understand at least one foreign language, and to communicate in it, at however modest a level, has an educational value'.[73] Of course one does not know what the authors of this Schools Council Working Paper mean by 'educational value'. But such an ability in itself does not betoken anything that I would recognise as educationally valuable. Secondly, a related point, it follows from the arguments deployed throughout this essay, that reference to the intellectual training that language study might provide would not constitute an adequate justification for its inclusion as a compulsory element.

Thirdly, although I would accept that a proper appreciation of French literature necessitates the ability to read French, and I regard French literature as being as valuable as any other, this argument cannot realistically be used to justify compulsory French. The vast majority of children do not attain to anything like the standard of competence necessary to reading French literature fluently. Since proper appreciation of French, or any other, literature also demands familiarity with the culture and historical setting from which it comes, and a wide acquaintance with the literature, time would be more profitably spent (so far as the literature is concerned) reading it in translation and studying French history.

Finally, although there is some value in being able to speak French for the individual, in that he can gain some satisfaction from this when he visits France, such a consideration seems altogether too negligible to warrant a share of the compulsory curriculum. Whatever need industry and commerce has for linguists can surely be supplied from those who choose to study the language, whether because they think they will enjoy it, or because they see it as necessary to the sort of job they want in industry or commerce.

The only consideration that gives me pause for thought is the suggestion that the ability to speak somebody else's language is obviously a great help to communication and increased understanding. Such a consideration must appeal to the utilitarian. But in practice, one reflects, the suggestion does not fulfil its promise: so few come to speak the language well enough to communicate; the ability to communicate with the French alone will not greatly increase world harmony and understanding; the fact that we can already communicate with the Americans does not seem to make a great deal of practical difference.

Latin, which may be taken as representative of all dead languages, gains a place as an option only because it is complex. Incidentally I do not count the fact that some may want to teach this or any other proposed option as a measure of 'relevance'. To do so would obviously constitute a circular argument: Latin is relevant to those who want to teach Latin to those to whom it will be relevant, because they will want to teach it, etc. (Perhaps this is an 'infinite' rather than a 'circular' argument. Anyway it is not a good one.) But I do count it as a minimal point in favour of Latin (and all other languages) that some specialists are needed for a full understanding of the literature (see above). Such a full understanding on the part of some is desirable for a full understanding of the history of the period and a faithful translation of literary texts. Every age, it has been said, needs its own translations of foreign literature. No age can have them if there are not some who understand the original tongue.

Latin is not classics, and it is worth noting in passing that the fact that classics as such is not mentioned in this essay does not necessarily mean that it is not in a sense studied. Taking classics to mean the study of the literature and history of ancient civilisations, there is no reason at all why such study should not constitute a part – an integrated part – of the study of literature and history.

Cooking, carpentry and typing are not very complex activities (which is not to impugn the skill of a good cook or skilled carpenter), nor is it obvious that a tutor would be as invaluable in these spheres as in some previously considered. On the other hand, though their claims may be relatively low on the criterion of complexity, they score well on the criterion of social utility which runs directly into the criterion of relevance in these cases. The point is that cooking, carpentry and typing represent examples of activities which it may be useful, or even necessary, for the individual to engage in anyway. Many people will have to cook and find themselves faced with carpentering jobs or typing needs; these are therefore useful skills for the individual to acquire from his own point of view. It is true that they can be picked up simply by practice, but that is no good reason for the school declining to offer them as options.

By contrast mountaineering, photography, angling and dancing, though they may be great sources of pleasure, besides not being particularly difficult to master, are neither useful nor relevant in my senses of those terms. They are predominantly private activities and what one might term 'extras' in life. To say as much is not to slight them. No doubt we all need some 'extras' in life; but then we all find them, through friends, societies, of our own accord, as offshoots of what we do in schools, or howsoever.

Once again it is crucial that it be understood that my argument does not involve the claim that angling is a less worthwhile pursuit than typing. The claim is simply (1) that given the nature of the society in which we live there is some value in providing students with the opportunity (and the time) to learn typing, and (2) assuming that we cannot do everything, there is less value in deploying resources on activities that only provide immediate pleasure to the agent, are not inherently difficult to master, and can be (and by definition are) engaged in without the help of the school.

V.   QUATERNARY STAGE

Philosophy

In proposing that philosophy should provide the culminating point of the curriculum I revert to an idea of Plato's. To him philosophy was the science of sciences, the supreme form of knowledge or the ultimate state of cognition.

Philosophers today tend to fight shy of such exalted claims for their discipline. Perhaps one of the most important reasons for this reticence is the widespread feeling that philosophy cannot produce the answers to many of the questions it succeeds in raising, and, in particular, that Plato was wrong to think that man could come to know the good and the evil by philosophy or any other means. I have argued elsewhere that, even if this latter claim be granted, there is still an important distinction to be made between moral experts, in the sense of those who understand the nature of the moral sphere and its problems, and those who, lacking in expertise, do not.[74] But here I am concerned only with reasserting the more general claim that philosophy is the supreme form of knowledge and that moral philosophy is its important branch. (I am using 'form of knowledge' in my sense of the term.)

In order to do this, I need first to clarify what I mean by 'philosophy' and then what I mean by 'supreme' or 'most important'. Just as Plato had to distinguish between dialectics or true philosophy and the antics of such sophists as Euthydemus,[75] so I must distinguish between true philosophy and the professional activity of certain lecturers in philosophy. Truth to tell, but sad to relate, the distinction is in many ways similar.

The most obvious characteristic of philosophy is passion for truth. Philosophy is concerned to discover what is true, and it therefore goes whither the argument leads. It is not concerned with confuting for the sake of display, refuting for the sake of an ideology, with virtuosity for the sake of success or prestige, or with argument designed to gain money, power or prestige. In this it differs from the activity of certain sophists and some so-called radical philosophers whose object is to change the world in the light of preconceived ideals.

Secondly philosophy is not to be identified with the ordinary-language definitions of a Prodicus or many modern analytic philosophers.[76] Of course there is a place for such activity, and the unwary may fail to see the distinction between the Prodican hair-splitting involved in eking out two senses of 'learning' and asking 'What is justice?' – the latter being a significant philosophical question – but it is not the whole or even the chief part of philosophy.[77] That chief part is rather, in Plato's terminology, knowledge of the Ideas.

Now this claim cannot simply be left standing there, since there are many obscurities and problems in Plato's theory of Ideas and many competent philosophers who frankly scorn it.[78] But at least one part of what Plato meant is both sure and sufficient to characterise the chief function of philosophy: namely that true understanding of science, the arts, mathematics, etc. is impossible without examination of the fundamental concepts, axioms and methodology of the discipline in question. The pursuit of such understanding is a philosophical task. Lest any reader think that this is a vulgar and trivial battle for pre-eminence amongst subjects, let me stress that I am not much concerned whether we call such an activity philosophy. My point is that such an enquiry related to, say, science is not the same thing as doing science, and so on through the other subjects. What I choose to call philosophy is this particular kind of activity which may be pursued in relation to any discipline.

All disciplines embody a system such that those familiar with the discipline can move about in that system. Thus the historian is familiar with a certain subject matter and certain rules and methods of procedure appropriate to an attempt to structure and understand his material. The same is true of the psychologist, sociologist, physicist and so on. But before it can be said with any degree of certainty that an historian has truly understood some event in the past or that a psychologist has correctly explained some aspect of human behaviour, we need something more than evidence that the individual historian or psychologist is competent within his system. The system itself needs to be examined and understood. We need to question the validity of its axioms, the nature of its evidence and the meaning of its terms. And we need answers to general questions such as what counts as 'truth' and what constitutes 'knowledge'. When a psychologist talks about 'unconscious motivation' we need to enquire whether that is not a contradiction in terms? What is he actually talking about? What is the nature of his evidence for talking about it? It is not for a non-historian to challenge an Hegelian interpretation of history as historically unsound, but it is part of philosophy's role to question the nature and validity of drawing determinist or historicist conclusions from such evidence as we have at all. The sort of questions I here refer to are those which are nowadays categorised as belonging to the philosophy of science, the philosophy of history, the philosophy of art, and so on. But it is clear that the fundamental questions in each of these branches of philosophy are questions about the nature of knowledge or epistemology. Thus I suggest the central concern of philosophy is the systematic pursuit of such questions as 'What is truth?' or 'What are the logical differences between different kinds of proposition?' In a word: epistemology.

The importance of such a study is obvious: to know what Hegel said, but not to appreciate the questionable basis on which his view of history is based, is not only not to know very much but also to be in grave danger of knowing more than is good for one. Similarly, to assume that the findings of a Freud or a Weber cannot properly be challenged except on empirical grounds by those who are experts in the same system is both false and potentially dangerous. A proper appreciation of the contribution to man's knowledge made by a Freud is dependent both on understanding his work from the point of view of psychology and on what I term a philosophic understanding of the nature of the activity itself.

Philosophy is supreme in the sense that it is logically ultimate. It comes, in plain words, last. There has to be history before there can be a philosophy of history, but both have to exist before we can talk of historical knowledge with any confidence. Philosophy is often referred to as a second-order discipline, which phrase – though perhaps mis-leading – I take to mean much what I am saying.

My second claim, again following Plato, is that moral philosophy is the most important branch of philosophy, which is to say that epistemo-logical questions related specifically to the moral sphere have the edge on epistemological questions related to other spheres. Plato's argument for this claim was tied up with a particular metaphysical view, ac-cording to which the whole cosmos is a rational structure and the Good in some sense literally governs and gives meaning to all reality. He was also wedded to the belief that certain knowledge was possible in relation to the Good. Neither of these tenets meets with much support today.

But even if we concede that we do not see the logical possibility of arriving at an indisputable moral truth, even if there are no fixed and certain answers in this sphere, it may still be true that enquiry into the sphere of morality, questions about the logical status of moral proposi-tions, consideration of morality from an epistemological point of view, is of supreme importance. And surely this is true. The question that theoretically matters most in the world is 'What matters and how do we know what matters?' That philosophy may not produce any in-contestable answers to such a question does not mean that the task of considering the question is not important. The truth is, as Plato in a more practical vein also pointed out,[79] that the matters on which people disagree to the point of violence and catastrophe are matters of value. Questions of value are thus of considerable practical import and they have a logical supremacy over questions of fact in that no amount of factual information can in itself determine or issue forth in any par-ticular action or behaviour. Man's ability to choose inescapably en-slaves him to value judgements.

My conclusion then, and my final curricular recommendation, is that all students should be initiated into philosophy, but since it would be wildly unrealistic to suppose that many will be capable of becoming competent philosophers or that any could proceed very far in a single year, I must add a more practical account of what I envisage.

The first objective would be to provide some awareness of this second form of knowledge – to get across the point that there are some questions that cannot be determined by empirical means. As a result of the pre-ceding stages of the curriculum there are three obvious areas to which this form of knowledge may be related: the moral, the aesthetic and the religious. Now is the time to consider and question the warrant, if any, for the moral attitudes that have been developed, to examine what kind of evidence, if any, might substantiate a religious interpretative attitude, and to enquire into the possibility of objectively valid aesthetic judgements. The emphasis would be, as it always is in philosophy, on critical questioning of widespread assumptions, but it would be an informed questioning, since it has been preceded by an initiation into the spheres in question. Thus subsumed under the first objective of promoting an awareness of the philosophical form of knowledge would be two more objectives : developing a critical attitude towards matters not embraced by the scientific form of knowledge, and, specifically, promoting an understanding of the epistemological problems in the spheres of art, religion and morality.

A fourth objective would be to indicate the problems inherent in the procedures of any or all of the elements included elsewhere in the curriculum, but particularly in the procedures of sociology and psychology. Neither of these disciplines, it will be remembered, has necessarily been studied as such by any individual, but many of the findings that will have been introduced as data in social studies will stem from sociological and psychological enquiry. The status of those findings is of considerable practical significance.

But why seek to impose this conspicuously theoretical and academic pursuit on all children? Is it that we should develop the rational mind, which by definition involves appreciation of the two basic forms of knowledge? No. Is it that truth is valuable in itself, and that such a pursuit is one necessary precondition of finding truth? No. The argument is this : philosophic understanding, of the type envisaged here, is a necessary condition of avoiding certain kinds of error; and those kinds of error are to be fought against on the grounds that they cause mischief, damage and harm. I shall now list some examples of the sorts of error I have in mind. (The list is in no particular order, and some examples are merely specific instances of a more general kind of error.)

The error of assuming that one can deduce that something ought to be the case simply from the fact that it is the case, or the error of confusing empirical and evaluative claims. The error of assuming that theory and practice are somehow quite independent of each other. The error of assuming that the basic axioms of things as diverse as Freudian psychology and Marxist sociology are beyond question. The error of assuming that what we do not know how to prove must be false, and, consequently, the specific error of assuming that it is incontestably true that religions are based on false superstitions. The similar error of assuming it to be known to be true that morality is just a matter of cultural inclination and the converse error of assuming it to be known to be true that there are certain objectively valid moral principles. The errors occasioned by succumbing to emotive language and by assuming arguments to be well-founded without having clarified the meaning of key concepts. The error of confusing explanation with justification.

These are merely select illustrative examples. The point is that errors of this sort can be seen every day to lead to unnecessary wrangles and disputes, can cause people to adopt opinions for which there is no warrant, and, *in extremis*, can lead to differences of opinion that issue forth in violent action. To rid the world of such errors, though it would not automatically lead to unanimity and peace, would be to remove a most potent source of pain. That is ultimately the justification of the pursuit of what I have termed philosophy.

VI CONCLUSION

In attempting to assess the desirability of any specific curriculum there are four things we have to do. First we have to consider whether, regardless of what it might achieve, there is anything that strikes us as immoral about it. Secondly we have to be convinced that it is practicable. Thirdly we have to understand exactly what it is that will be achieved by the curriculum. And finally we have to ask ourselves whether there is good reason to regard whatever will be achieved as desirable.

I can see no grounds for maintaining that there is anything immoral about this curriculum. The only charge that I can conceive of that might be raised against it on this score would be that it is wrong to compel children to do what they do not initially want to do. That charge has, I hope, been sufficiently answered in the previous pages.[80]

I have not, I admit, proved that it is practicable, but I see absolutely no reason why it should not be, especially since the curriculum put forward allows of considerable latitude and experimentation in respect of method. The only strings attached so far as methodology goes are those that are logically demanded by the objectives of the exercise: thus it is necessary that whatever methods of teaching or organisation of the curriculum are involved they should not obscure the distinction between what I have termed scientific and philosophical questions. Similarly, given the object of the exercise, it is necessary that the initiation into science should take some form that allows the child to appreciate, at an appropriate level, what it is to do science, rather than simply be fed with scientific data. Apart from that kind of consideration, no statements on methodology accompany the curriculum. That means not only that the way is open to argue for specific kinds of integration, team-teaching, discovery-learning in some particular sense, and so on, but also that a case might be made for adopting different approaches with different children. A uniform content does not necessarily imply a uniform methodology. Given this lack of dogmatism, it is very difficult to believe that it must prove impossible to introduce the vast majority of children to this content.

What will exposure to this content achieve? If an individual were to experience this curriculum and successfully attain to the various objectives that the elements, both separately and taken as a whole, were designed to meet, what would he have acquired, what would he be, as a result of his schooling?

He would be physically healthy and aware of how to retain that health, in so far as such things are in the individual's control. He would be numerate and literate, which skills would be of some use to him in everyday life and serve as means to a variety of further ends.

Intellectually, attitudes of perseverance, concern for evidence, and consistency, and skills of memorising, hypothesising and deducing would have been cultivated. The main vehicle for the cultivation of such qualities will have been history, but he would also be aware of the distinction between two fundamental forms of knowledge, as well as having some familiarity with the nature of certain important and distinguishable disciplines: science and mathematics he would have met by direct experience, and through what I have termed philosophy he would have given consideration also to such things as sociology and psychology. He would not necessarily be experienced or competent in these disciplines, but he would understand something of what they were about and something of the problems inherent in them.

He would be habitually inclined to consider other people's welfare and would be well-informed about the actual condition of the society in which he lives. But any tendency to dogmatic and intolerant fanaticism in respect of his moral beliefs would be tempered by an understanding of the puzzling status of moral judgements. A related point is that he would appreciate the existence of rival interpretative attitudes and be familiar with various specific examples of the religious attitude. He might or might not subscribe to some religious interpretative attitude himself, but, if he did, he would have no excuse for regarding it as unquestionably valid, and, if he did not, he would have no excuse for scorning those who did as in some way intellectually lacking.

More generally he would be cosmopolitan rather than provincial in outlook, appreciative of the diversity and complexity of human nature and social practice, as a result of his studies in history and literature. He would have the open and questioning mind that we hear so much about today. But in this instance, which is unusual, we can see how it would have been developed and that it would have been developed alongside a necessary acquisition of information and competence. Where others propose that the curriculum should consist simply of children asking and answering questions as they feel inclined, without any reference to information, competence, awareness of alternative views or, more generally, the quality of the questions and answers, this curriculum enables individuals to detect nonsense.[81]

Finally he would be skilled in those activities that he had chosen to be skilled in, his choices having been made with at least some degree of understanding. He would be as well prepared for a job suited to his talents and interests as it is possible for anyone to be in an imperfect world. So far as pursuits other than his job went, he would similarly be in a position to make a choice that is not foredoomed by lack of understanding. Certainly he may turn his back on the so-called higher culture. But in scorning the fine arts he would not be scorning what he did not understand or cutting himself off from what might have been a source of pleasure had he but been given a little guidance.

Such a portrait is of course highly idealised. This curriculum is not going to be altogether effective and it is not going to produce a noticeably higher proportion of saints than any other curriculum. But the argument is that such is the nature of the curriculum that one would expect it to make some sort of tangible contribution to the sort of result outlined.

It will be rightly observed that there is nothing particularly original or bizarre about this curriculum. This may worry my publisher, but it does not worry me. Despite the heavy emphasis on divergent and lateral thinking in some quarters, who actually wants to be different for the sake of being different? I, for one, am much more interested in attempting to approximate to the truth than to the novel – more concerned to do what there seems good reason to do than what nobody else has done before.

It is true, in particular, that this curriculum owes a lot to P. H. Hirst and J. P. White. I have taken over ideas that I first found in their published work and my actual curricular proposals are not dissimilar to theirs. But it is important to stress the differences (just as it is important to stress the differences between each of them). For, according to my argument, even those elements which are common to all three curricula cannot be justified on either of their terms.

Science, for instance, is, as White says, a complex activity, but that alone cannot justify its inclusion in the curriculum, since, despite White's contrary claim, there is no reason to suppose that it is any more complex or difficult to understand than transcendental meditation, which is not included in his curriculum. Similarly the items that Hirst classifies as forms of knowledge all find their way into my curriculum, but not on the grounds that they are forms of knowledge, which I dispute. Because my reasons for including them vary from item to item, it is legitimate for me to argue that some of them should take up different amounts of time.

This curriculum introduces the individual to what I have termed the two forms of knowledge, the two interpretative attitudes, and four basic kinds of awareness. (If there is an historical kind of awareness, it also introduces the individual to that.) In the course of this chapter, I have not made a great deal of reference to these classifications, since the various elements can for the most part be justified without reference to them. But now it may be added that the curriculum may be justified schematically, on utilitarian terms, by reference to these classifications.

Insofar as people have understanding of the two forms, the two interpretative attitudes and the four kinds of awareness, so far are they in a position to cope appropriately with logically distinct kinds of question, to tolerate rather than dismiss alternative interpretative attitudes, and to gain satisfaction from, as well as to appreciate in others, concern for the various types of awareness. They are in a position to do this. They will not necessarily do so. But if they lack such understanding they cannot possibly do so. If they cannot do so, we must resign ourselves to a community in which people do not understand one another, base their opinions and arguments on fundamental logical mistakes and ignorance, and are incapable of responding to or appreciating in others one or more of the distinct kinds of sentiment of which human beings are capable. The objection to this state of affairs is that it will make for a miserable life.

The curriculum is for our time and something like our society. It would not necessarily be worthwhile for another time and another place. If, for example, there were a society that were able to thrive and in which people were happy, without any contact with this materialistic and industrial world, and without recourse to science as we know it, then by my argument, there would be no case for trying to introduce the study of science in such a community. But there is no such society, and, if there is, it is not ours.

It will be noted also that this curriculum does not guarantee, or even seek to ensure, that individuals will come as adults to devote their lives to a selection of the most worthwhile activities. Thus, although it must be that, as things are, literature is in itself more worthwhile than bingo, if the majority of individuals end up preferring bingo, then they shall play it. The curriculum only seeks to ensure that they choose it because it is more pleasurable to them, and not because it is all that they are able to do. At the same time the curriculum does seek to ensure that some individuals will want to pursue activities that are particularly worthwhile in that they have great instrumental value in promoting pleasure for the community as a whole, such as science. And it does seek to ensure that no individual will want to pursue activities that are positively worthless in that they cause pain to others.

Perhaps the single most important point to stress is that a utilitarian curriculum is more concerned with the development of certain intellectual qualities, cognitive abilities, attitudes and understanding, than it is with gratifying instincts, providing useful but simple skills, or merely concentrating on the immediate pleasure of the child. And this for a very simple reason : if we are really concerned about enabling individuals to find as much satisfaction for themselves as they possibly could, while participating in a community that is itself happy in such a way as to contribute to the general pleasure, if we are really concerned about this as an ideal in the real world, then knowing how to mend a fuse, understanding economics, being stuck through lack of capability rather than choice at the level of bingo, and so on are either useless or positively antagonistic to the aim.

If pain is to be diminished in the world, then what is primarily needed is tolerance, sympathy and reason. This curriculum does not offer these commodities on a plate. No curriculum could. But it seeks to provide the understanding, intellectual and emotional, the awareness and the wideness of outlook that are in practice necessary to them.

So the final question is whether the sort of outlook, information, ability, state of mind and opportunity for informed choice that this curriculum is designed to promote is desirable or worthwhile. My contention is simple : such a curriculum is worthwhile because, insofar as the objectives are met, it will increase the chances of the individual finding a maximum of pleasure for himself, while at the same time developing all individuals in such a way as to increase the likelihood of pleasure in the community as a whole. I can think of no other ultimate consideration that would render this or any other curriculum desirable. I can think of no other kind of curriculum that would be as likely to achieve this aim. QED.

Notes and references

1 J. P. White, *Towards a Compulsory Curriculum*, op. cit.
2 D. Aspin, 'Ethical Aspects of Sport, Games and Physical Education', in *Proc. Phil. Ed. Soc. G.B.*, vol. 9, 1975. This paper was delivered at the Annual Conference of the Philosophy of Education Society, Christmas, 1974. P. Renshaw's companion paper, 'On Distinguishing between Physical Activities', was also delivered at that conference. For some inexplicable reason it was not subsequently published by the Society.
3 J. May, 'Physical Education', in R. C. Whitfield, *Disciplines of the Curriculum*, op. cit., p. 203.
4 D. Anthony, 'Is there a future for P.E.?' in *The Times Educational Supplement*, 16 Feb. 1971, p. 31.
5 W. F. Updike, P. B. Johnson, *Principles of Modern Physical Education, Health and Recreation* (Holt, Rinehart & Winston, 1970).

6   G. H. Bantock, 'Towards a Theory of Popular Education', in R. Hooper (ed.), *The Curriculum*, op. cit., p. 263.

7   R. S. Peters, *Ethics and Education*, op. cit.

8   In my *Plato, Utilitarianism and Education*, op. cit.

9   e.g. *Plato, Utilitarianism and Education*, op. cit, and *Moral Philosophy for Education*, op. cit., ch. 14.

10 I. Berlin, preface to M. Yudkin (ed.), *General Education* (Penguin, 1971), p. 9.

11 P. H. Nidditch, 'Philosophy of Education and the Place of Science in the Curriculum', in G. Langford and D. J. O'Connor (eds), *New Essays in the Philosophy of Education* (Routledge & Kegan Paul, 1973).

12 P. H. Nidditch, op. cit., p. 252.

13 Ibid., p. 251.

14 Ibid., p. 252.

15 Ibid., p. 253.

16 Ibid., p. 253.

17 Ibid., p. 252.

18 See above, Ch. 2.iii.

19 M. Yudkin, 'Experimental Science', in M. Yudkin (ed.), *General Education*, op. cit.

20 Ibid., p. 138.

21 R. C. Whitfield (ed.), *Disciplines of the Curriculum*, op. cit., p. 1.

22 M. Yudkin, op. cit., p. 138.

23 Ibid., p. 158.

24 B. Ritchie, 'Physics', in R. C. Whitfield (ed.), op. cit., p. 127.

25 See below, Part D.

26 S. Nisbet, *Purpose in the Curriculum*, op. cit., pp. 93ff. on science.

27 Ibid., p. 96.

28 See above, Ch. 2.iii.

29 P. H. Nidditch, op. cit., p. 254.

30 B. Ritchie, in R. C. Whitfield (ed.), op. cit., ch. 10.

31 J. Eggleston, 'Biology', in R. C. Whitfield (ed.), op. cit., ch. 12.

32 E. Coulson, 'Chemistry', in R. C. Whitfield (ed.), op. cit., ch. 11, p. 143.

33 J. Eggleston, op. cit., p. 158.

34 See above, Ch. 2.vii, and R. F. Dearden, *The Philosophy of Primary Education*, op. cit., and J. P. White, *Towards a Compulsory Curriculum*, op. cit.

35 A. Tayler, A. Tammadge and P. Prescott, 'Mathematics', in M. Yudkin (ed.), op. cit., p. 96.

36 Ibid., p. 133.

37 S. Nisbet, op. cit., p. 86.

38 A. Bishop, 'Mathematics', in R. C. Whitfield (ed.), op. cit.

39 Ibid., p. 121.

40 See above, Ch. 2.iii.

41 In *Plato, Utilitarianism and Education*, op. cit., I attempted to defend the indoctrination of the *Republic* in the ideal circumstances there envisaged.

42 'Christianity, Buddhism and Marxism' are singled out on the grounds that they are religions with a considerable following.

43 H. Marratt, 'Religious Education', in R. C. Whitfield (ed.), op. cit., ch. 3, p. 48.

44 See, e.g., Q. Bell, 'Fine Arts', in J. H. Plumb (ed.), *Crisis in the Humanities* (Penguin, 1964)..

45 D. Field, 'Art', in R. C. Whitfield (ed.), op. cit., ch. 13, p. 168.

46 See above, Ch. 2.vii.

47 J. H. Plumb, 'The Historian's Dilemma', in J. H. Plumb (ed.), *Crisis in the Humanities*, op. cit., p. 28.
48 Ibid., p. 37.
49 Ibid., p. 42.
50 J. L. Heydon, 'History', in M. Yudkin (ed.), op. cit.
51 Ibid., p. 53.
52 S. Nisbet, op. cit., p. 89; said of social studies in which he includes history.
53 M. Booth, 'History', in R. C. Whitfield (ed.), op. cit., ch. 5, p. 73.
54 G. Hough, 'Crisis in Literary Education', in J. H. Plumb (ed.), op. cit.
55 Ibid., pp. 99 and 101.
56 Ibid., p. 99.
57 Ibid., p. 107.
58 R. Bower, 'English', in M. Yudkin (ed.), op. cit.
59 See William Morris, *News from Nowhere* (Routledge and Kegan Paul, 1970).
60 F. R. Leavis, 'Sociology and Literature', in *The Common Pursuit* (Penguin, 1972).
61 J. P. White, op. cit., p. 46.
62 R. G. Woods and R. Barrow, *Introduction to the Philosophy of Education*, op. cit., p. 178.
63 A. and E. Gissing (eds.), *Letters of George Gissing to his Family* (Constable, 1927), p. 83.
64 Ibid., p. 128.
65 See, e.g., H. Rosen, 'Language and Class', in D. Holly (ed.), *Education or Domination?*, op. cit.
66 D. Holly, 'The Invisible Ruling Class', in *Education or Domination?*, op. cit., p. 107.
67 The phrase comes from W. Labov, 'The Logic of Non-standard English', in P. Giglioli (ed.), *Language and Social Context* (Penguin, 1972), p. 171.
68 R. C. Whitfield (ed.), op. cit., p. 7.
69 Provided that it is not gained at the expense of others.
70 H. J. Mackinder, 'On the Scope and Methods of Geography', in *Proc. Royal Geog. Soc.*, vol. 60, 1887.
71 E. W. Gilbert, 'The Idea of the Region', in *Geography*, 45, pt 5, 1960.
72 R. Hartshorne, *Perspectives on the Nature of Geography* (Chicago, 1959).
73 'The Development of Modern Language Teaching in Secondary Schools', Schools Council Working Paper, no. 19, HMSO, 1969.
74 See my 'Who are the Philosopher-Kings?', in *Proc. Phil. Ed. Soc. G.B.*, vol. 8, no. 2, July 1974, and my 'What's Wrong with the Philosophy of Education?', in *B.J.E.S.*, vol. 22, no. 2, June 1974.
75 See Plato, *Euthydemus*.
76 The sophist Prodicus is referred to in passing in various Platonic dialogues. To do him justice, see W. K. C. Guthrie, *The Sophists* (Cambridge University Press, 1971).
77 For a still important, if somewhat intemperate, attack on much of what passes for philosophy from Wittgenstein to the present day, see E. Gellner, *Words and Things* (Gollancz, 1959).
78 On Plato's theory of ideas, see G. C. Field, *The Philosophy of Plato* (Oxford, 1969), chs 1 and 2.
79 e.g. Plato, *Euthyphro*, 7.D.
80 See above, Ch. 2.iv.
81 The reader will recognise, I feel sure, the implied reference to N. Postman and C. Weingartner, *Teaching as a Subversive Activity* (Penguin, 1969).

Index